You're Pregnant Too, Mate!

You're Pregnant Too, Mate!

Gavin Rodgers

Robson Books

First published in Great Britain in 1999 by Robson Books,
10 Blenheim Court, Brewery Road, London N7 9NT

A member of the Chrysalis Group plc

British Library Cataloguing in Publication Data
A catalogue record for this title is available from the
British Library

ISBN 1 86105 277 4

Typeset by SX Composing DTP, Rayleigh, Essex
Printed and bound by Creative Print and Design, Ebbw Vale

Contents

To Bernadette, for bearing me
children and bearing me

Introduction:
Man to Man

Introductions

Pregnancy is one of the most intense experiences of anyone's life and throws up a thousand questions for the parents. There are plenty of books around for expectant mothers, but virtually nothing for the expectant father . . . Yeah, yeah . . . Blah, blah, blah . . .

This is the bit of the book you're thinking of skipping. Am I right? It's hard enough to find time to even open a book what with all that essential TV that needs watching. You still have those Christmas videos to catch up on: *100 Greatest Slide Tackles* and Jim Bowen's *Bullseye* uncut – including 75 minutes too hot for TV. Even if you like books, why waste effort on the wordy preamble?

And it's not just books. Introductions of any sort tend to be awkward.

You go into a pub one night, a stag night, say. You don't know anyone except the groom and you don't like him very much – he just happens to be marrying your sister.

First thing the groom does is introduce you to his five best pals. Several 'all rights' and 'hello, mates' are bandied about while everyone including you wishes you hadn't bothered to show up. A couple of blokes shake your hand which gets messed up either because you shook hands too soft or too hard or so clumsily a

1

couple of fingers got dislocated. Names are mentioned, of course. They must have been anyway, but the stress of the situation meant you were never able to hear them, let alone remember them. It genuinely crosses your mind to say you're nipping out for some fags and then scarper.

Four hours later, you feel you've known these same six blokes since they were born. You know their names, their personalities, what they drink, how they drink, which one had his first sexual experience with his sister's pet rabbit Snowy, which one has a criminal record for 'borrowing' cars, who's on the pull, who wants a fight, etc. etc.

Everything now is relaxed and easy. You still don't like the bloke who's marrying your sister, particularly as there's a good chance he has myxomatosis. But if only you could have avoided all that awkward introductory, conversationy stuff. You can actually, but you have to drink several scotches before you go out. Unfortunately everyone then thinks you are an alcoholic. Worse still, they are correct.

So all you alcoholics can skip this bit and move straight to the first chapter. The rest must stay behind for this get-to-know-you session. Think of it as a first team squad pre-season get-together. Later in the week we're taking a coach trip to see *Phantom of the Opera*, followed by a twelve-in-a-bed orgy at the local Moat House hotel.

So, if you're ready, let's try again.

Introduction (Take Two)

Pregnancy is one of the most intense experiences of anyone's life and throws up a thousand questions for the parents. There are plenty of books around for expectant mothers, but virtually nothing for the expectant father. A survey of your local book shop reveal guides for first time mums, second time mums, single mums, working mums and even lesbian mums (okay, I made that last one up). Look a bit harder and there's pregnancy books for grandparents, sisters, and even best friends. You don't want to make fuss, but aren't we forgetting someone here?

Roughly three quarters of a million babies are born to women in the UK every year. It's fair to assume at least some of them even have fathers.

You're Pregnant Too, Mate! is a complete guide through pregnancy for the expectant father. Your wife or partner almost certainly wants you to take an active interest in what's going on.

You are happy to oblige but that six-hundred-page text-book beside the bed entitled something like *Know Your Own Cervix* or *Vagina Britannica* is not your idea of a fun read.

This guide, *You're Pregnant Too, Mate!* is aimed at you, the ordinary bloke. You want to be involved and you want be an effective birthing partner but you want to enjoy it while you learn. You enjoyed learning how to make a baby, why should the sequel be any different?

The Nine-Nine-Nine Months

Men get pregnant too.

Not physically; you don't binge on weird foods, throw up in the mornings or suffer dizzy spells. Not unless the hangover is really bad. Neither do you get irritable, go off sex and blimp up twice your size – that comes later, after you've been married a few years.

What I mean is, you too have to go through nine exciting but terrifying months. You are expected to have instant solutions to your partner's morning sickness, breast engorgement and varicose veins. You must comfort and reassure her through a million crises and cravings. Cruel and unusual tasks face you like perusing puddles of broken waters or midnight redecoration of the nursery. You are, in effect, her twenty-four hour a day medical and emotional helpline. You might wish you could just extend her RAC cover, but you can't.

So who is there to help you? Plenty of people. Medical teams are always on alert. You'll be instructed, you'll be cared for, you'll be pampered. And when it's all over everyone says: well done, hero, take a hard-earned rest, here's flowers and balloons and chocolates and grapes and . . . Oh no, they don't. That's all for the mother. You, the birthing assistant, might well feel like just a poor drudge running and fetching for the main attraction.

Why Men Need a Guide

Attitudes to men in pregnancy have always been mixed. Take a black and white 1950s film I saw recently on TV. There was a scene where a nurse is startled by a man in the hospital grounds. She recognises him.

'Mr Jones, what on earth are you doing out here in the middle of the night?'

'Sorry, matron, it's my wife, you see. She's having twins and

I was on my way to the maternity ward to see if there's any news.'

'Come, come, Mr Jones, if your wife is having twins, the last place they'll want you is the maternity ward. Run along now.'

'Yes, matron. Sorry, matron.'

That's right, they both knew the maternity ward was the *last* place he should be.

As little as forty years ago this 'certain condition' was regarded as something a woman handled alone and very much in private. Her pregnancy would never be mentioned by the prospective father, and only tentatively by her friends or sisters. Even her mother.

'Annie, we need to talk. Have you sat on a dirty toilet seat recently?'

'Yes, Mum *(sob)*. I have, Mum *(sob)*. Not only that, I've been shagging my boyfriend to kingdom come.'

A man's role was restricted to nervously pacing the hall at home listening to the heavy click of the grandfather clock, perhaps wondering if afterbirth tasted any better than bully-beef.

Back then, a working man never even got the day off for the birth of his child. At the onset of labour he would run up to the phone box to call 999. He might be allowed to ride in the ambulance but was turfed out at the gates of the hospital, probably with a stern flea in his ear from matron. A kiss for luck and that was that. That he might witness the birth never entered his thoughts. If, in some brainstorm, he asked to cut the cord, they would probably have said yes, and you can tie the noose and sling it across the branch as well if you like, you sick pervert.

The 1950s man could not return to hospital until the next visiting day, which would probably be a Sunday and their child already a few days old.

'Excuse me, matron, may I see the baby now?'

'Very well, then. You can peer through the nursery window. Yours is the fifth one from the right, I believe. Can't miss it, though, bit of a runt with sticky-out ears like yours . . . One warning, if you so much as touch the glass with your grubby little hands, I shall kick your goolies so far up you'll look like you have mumps.'

'Thank you, matron. This is the happiest day of my life.'

These days it seems perfectly normal for a man to not just attend the birth but to actively assist in it. The father is expected to guide his partner through pre-natal care, support her through labour, help her breathe, hold a leg, cut the cord and, if you're handy with a soldering iron, sort out putting her private parts back together. Much further and midwives won't just be underpaid, they'll be obsolete.

Certainly some men don't fancy it. The only advice they need is what shoes are most comfortable for the nervous pacing, or tips on forelock-tugging whenever someone in a white coat shows up. The maternity ward really is the last place they want to be.

But most men welcome these changes. Witnessing your children being born is an extremely rewarding experience, perhaps not quite on a par with finishing T-cutting your car, but mighty close.

Advice Squad

You're Pregnant Too, Mate! will navigate you throughout the pregnancy. Right from how to impregnate someone if you're having trouble (the book assumes you already have someone willing to participate – this is not *Seven Sure-fire Secrets of Becoming a Totty Magnet*) to coping with the emotional trauma of seeing your wife in pain, bleeding and birthing. (A couple of pints and pair of splash-proof goggles normally do the trick.)

In between there's advice on celebrating the news of pregnancy, wetting the baby's head after the birth and if I can think of any other excuse to get a few down you I'll put that in too . . . What do you reckon? First time her waistline gets bigger than yours must be worth cracking open a bottle of champagne.

Serious technical stuff is dealt with wherever necessary. After all, you want to be able to hold your own when the subject comes up.

'I gather your wife's seven months pregnant.'

'Yep, nearly halfway now.'

'Are you thinking of going for a Caesar?'

'Sod that rabbit food. I'm having a steak.'

You're Pregnant Too, Mate! will also give you some idea what to expect after the baby is born. By then your relationship will have changed. Your partner will not be the same person, and nor will you . . .

Pause a second at the hallway mirror. There you go, dashing off to the golf club in your slick suit, travelling there in your flash two-seater sports car. You're young, you're keen, the boss has high hopes for you. (Perhaps you'll even break a hundred one day.) Look again and savour your reflection while you can. In forty weeks' time you'll be lugging a buggy; a carry-cot complete with various blankets, pillows, rattles and mobiles; a fully stocked nappy-changing bag; and a three-foot-high purple fluffy dinosaur.

As you pass the mirror you won't even notice you have a stripe of yellow sick down your right shoulder. In fact you'll have had so little sleep you won't even care. And when you get outside, you'll notice two things. Firstly, it's dark, because it's taken you that long to get ready and secondly, your bijou racing green MG has been stolen – stolen by the heavy burden of new fatherhood. And in its place is a nine-year-old Volvo Estate. A beige Volvo Estate. It's got rust problems too. In fact the trendiest thing about it is the yellow plastic diamond stuck on the back window: Baby On Board . . . as if that wasn't obvious.

An Essential Guide

There's no running away from pregnancy – it wouldn't be right and frankly you're not fit enough. But as long as you read *You're Pregnant Too, Mate!* you won't even want to. It's a genuine pregnancy guide, just like she has, but directed towards the male half of the equation. (Yes, half!) It addresses your concerns. It also helps you to understand your partner's. This book will help you to help her and also help you to help yourself. At last someone is one hundred per cent on your side.

Okay, a hundred per cent is unrealistic. But I can do you sixty-five per cent. That's guaranteed. With no strings attached.

Very few strings. Thin ones. Threads, really.

Hold on, I've got it. I'll be on your side until the Fat Lady sprogs.

1

Conception: Sometimes a Sticky Problem

A Norwegian Would

Let's start with what you already know about babies. That's easily covered. You know nothing, zilch, sod all; you're Norway in the Eurovision Song Contest. When it comes to babies you live by a fjord, wear a hat with horns and think 'Jigga-Jig-Jig, I love Stig' comprises a hit single.

Hardly surprising with your attitude. Last time you came across a baby was last summer when your mate brought round his wife and newborn. You glanced in the crib and then announced with a chuckle, 'Poor little bleeder, turned out ugly as his dad', before following it up with, 'Right then, shall us lads make ourselves scarce in a pub-wards direction?'

Faced with a subject you knew nothing about, you gave it precisely eleven seconds of your attention.

The fact is you have a deficiency. You have no idea how to deal with babies. You don't know how to act around them or speak to them. Neither do you know how to hold them, pick them up, put them down. Until recently this has not been a problem, but now the prospect of having children yourself has arisen.

What's worse is you have a sneaking feeling this difficulty may be permanent. You're a personable enough bloke and like to think you can get on with most people. But whenever you've had to deal with babies . . .

Back to last summer. Your mate suggested that you might spend a bit of time with the newborn before going to the boozer. You agreed readily. (Quietly you were wondering if he had joined some weird sect.)

He suggested further that you might want to hold the bairn. You shrugged. You chuckled confidently. You bent towards the crib . . . then hesitated.

'Right ho, no problem, but how does one actually . . . ? Is there any particular . . . ? It won't break, will it?'

Your mate reassured you it wouldn't break. And picking it up was straightforward. Head at the top, legs at the bottom, basic-ally nothing to it. Obviously you had to be careful.

So you were careful, *bloody* careful . . . but the thing cried any-way. You immediately tried to hand it back to your mate but he told you not to worry. Hold him for a bit. Get to know each other.

Get to know each other? What were you supposed to do, tell it a couple of dirty jokes? Ask it how its pram was running? No, that wouldn't do. But you had no idea what would.

So you conclude: you and babies just don't mix.

Fortunately there's no need to worry. You are not alone in this attitude. It's not your fault. Virtually every bloke feels like this.

The reason is, none of us gets any training in babies. Getting On With Dribbly People Under Two Foot Tall was never an option at GCSE. Neither have you had much opportunity to enter the world of babies.

But the information is there inside you. Deep down you know what to do. You just need reminding.

If you don't believe me, it's worth remembering that you, many moons ago, were a baby yourself. You come from a long line of babies.

Single To Pluto, Please

Somehow women seem perfectly comfortable with babies. When your partner picked it up it didn't cry (and she wasn't half as careful as you were). Neither did she seem bothered with its incomprehensible conversation style. She chatted away quite happily to it.

Perhaps women *did* do it at school. They covered all that stuff: cooking without a microwave, caring about sock colour, being friendly to people with facial disfigurements. They must have done babies too.

But women get no formal training on babies and how to look after them. They can bluff their way through a visit from your mate, but that's about it. Truth be known they're as scared as you are.

The difference is they give the subject slightly more than eleven seconds of their attention. A possible reason for this attentiveness may be because from an early age they know what a woman has to go through to produce a baby. Becoming a mother means facing the mother-of-all excretions. (Thrashing about under the covers with a sweaty, pissed-up, twelve-stone man is the easy part.)

Just think if it was you who had to expel something the size of a rugby ball through the organ you've only previously employed for peeing. You'd be absolutely terrified. You'd have your entire groin sewn up and emigrate to Jupiter.

At what age this terrifying revelation dawns on a girl is any-one's guess. The chances are that the thunderbolt strikes around the time of their first period. A dribble in the knickers at twelve might well be the first subconscious inkling that one day they have to pass not just a great flood, but Noah, his ark, and several sets of oars as well.

Us chaps have a small initiation ceremony around the same

time. But the significance of our balls dropping may have been lost. Plink-plink. 'Hey guys, my balls just dropped. Now I get to have a deep, manly voice.'

So a woman has received some psychological information. And this helps. But not too much. If she looks totally comfortable around a baby, it's because she feels she should.

As I said before, don't worry if you don't understand babies. The only baby you need to understand is your own. Rest assured that you will. When you get it home you can draw the curtains and practise on it, picking it up, putting it down, burbling at it like a constipated orang-utan. And by the time your friends come round, you'll look halfway like you know what you're doing.

Your Central Reservation

The life you and your partner have now is absolutely fine. You have enough money and a lot of freedom. Why change it?

You've got nothing against babies. You're not prejudiced. Your mind couldn't be more open to the idea. But over the dinner table after a couple of glasses of wine you've been known to wonder aloud: 'Why the hell would I want to spend the rest of my born days living with a screaming brat and surrounded by seventeen tons of smelly nappies?'

Why indeed? But if we examine your heartfelt expression of doubt a little closer, you have actually expressed both of the main fears about babies: nappy changing and crying.

Firstly, young babies' dirty nappies have almost no smell. Breastfed babies' nappies are 100 per cent odourless. That's the honest truth. If you drank only milk, your pooh wouldn't smell too bad either. Pooh has gotten a bad name because you're basing your opinion of it on a guy who lives on lager and curry. Admittedly milk-pooh doesn't look too brilliant, and you wouldn't want to dab it behind your ears, but there's hardly any of it and it has very little aroma.

Once babies start eating solids at about eight months their nappy contents get a bit more serious, but we're talking about rabbit droppings here, not shed-loads of shire horse crap.

Disposable nappies are a doddle to change. Old one off, quick wipe, new one on. You can even buy a packet of tailor-made little orange plastic sacks to dispose of them into. Just pop the dirty nappy into one and tie a bow. It's like something gift wrapped from Harrods. The orange nappy-sacks are even perfumed, which is more than you can say for that jock-strap that's been festering under the bed for the last six months.

You might be thinking I've skipped over the fact that you actually have to wipe the bum of another human being. That is, risk getting Someone Else's Pooh on your pretty little hands. Yes, it happens, just like it does when you wipe your own bum. The solution is the same – soap and water, give your hands a quick wash and away you go. If you're about to share a taramasalata dip with someone you might want to be that bit extra thorough, but it really is that simple. After the SEP event has happened a few times you won't even think about it.

Babies do cry, some a lot, some very little. Other people's crying children may drive you around bend, but you'll cope much better when you love the baby as your own child. Never underestimate the power of that bond. Even if you end up with a screamer, he or she will be *your* screamer. You'll be boasting to the neighbours: 'Listen to my kid yell, eh? Lungs like Pavarotti but weighs less than his underpants . . . And, by the way, you should have seen the stupendous turd he produced in his potty this morning. I'm thinking of having it mounted.'

Life On the Hard Shoulder

Unassuaged by these revelations, you pour yourself another goblet of Bulgarian Merlot and press on. All right then, you say, forget the nappies and the screaming, what kind of a world is this to bring a baby into?

'A bloke in the pub was telling me about this survey, right. It was in the paper, right. Eighty-seven per cent of today's babies will end up as AIDS-infested drug addicts so riddled with BSE they'll be injecting crack into their own udders . . . It may have been 37 per cent.'

More wine.

'And before you say, "What's so awful about that?", it gets worse. This bloke reckoned, right, faced with global pollution, mass unemployment and pay-per-view Premiership football, a kid's best hope of happiness was to be the last remaining survivor of a nuclear holocaust.'

More wine.

'And this bloke was an optimist . . .'

More wine.

'He was. I promise.'

More wine.

'What do you mean, I'm slurring?'

Grey Import

What about the population explosion? Let's do some serious number crunching here.

Since 1981 the UK population has risen by about 8 per cent from 55 million to around 60 million. That increase is due entirely to people living longer. Birth rate is falling. If you want statistics, the proportion of people aged 75 and above rose 55 per cent. The proportion of people aged 0 to 4 years (babies) fell 15 per cent.

Add to this the recent estimation of life span stretching to 130 years and your conclusion is obvious. Far from a baby boom, we have a wrinkly boom.

This geriatrics glut could mean concepts such as 'middle age' will have to be completely rescheduled to a later date. In a couple of decades the new buzz-phrase will be 'Life begins at 90'. Callow youths of forty-five and fifty years old will be liable to carry switch-blades and spray graffiti on bus shelters: 'Terry Wogan Funks Me Up'; 'Got Viagra Running Around My Brain'.

Tony Blair's Cool Britannia will have become Blue Rinse Britannia. Viewed from a satellite, the UK will look like a stooped old lady, with Eire as her shopping trolley and the white cliffs of Dover a giant pair of incontinence pants.

The next millennium will see the trendy brasseries of Soho and Covent Garden thronging with white-haired, safari-suited, coffin-dodgers. 'I'll have a skinny, double shot of Ovaltine and a mashed potato croissant, please.'

The only solution is to have more babies.

The only other solution is to import the Dutch euthanasia laws. They go roughly along the lines of: if your grandmother coughs twice in a morning you can call in the council to forcibly administer a lethal injection.

Save Ounces

Another good reason to procreate is because babies pay tax , lots of it, hundred of thousands of pounds over their lifetime. Those tax pounds will largely be spent financing your expensive, extended retirement. In the span between sixty and a hundred and thirty you are going to wear out half a dozen Stannah stair-lifts and probably hundreds of zimmer frames.

Of course you could finance all this yourself, as the government wants, by upping your pension contributions. By the time

12

you've increased them to the requisite level you'll have about enough disposable income left from your wages to afford a packet of crisps.

You have two options:

1 Spend a couple of hours in the company of some seventeen-year-old spotty-necked financial adviser who will sell you a Personal Pension Plan tailor-made for your particular situation – before driving away in his commission-financed Ferrari 355.

2 Spend three minutes playing dip the chipolata with your nearest and dearest.

I know which one I would choose.

Psychological Tick

But all this hell and mayhem will not be brightening up our lives for sometime yet. In the meantime your partner tells you her biological clock is ticking away. You reply that it's probably running a bit fast because it's the one you bought her in the Argos sale last Christmas Eve. Why doesn't she hit the snooze button and have a childless lie-in for a couple more years?

She replies that it may not be a biological clock at all. But it does tick and is set to go off any time.

According to doctors, a woman is in her best shape physically to bear a child in her early twenties. After thirty-five the chances of her getting pregnant are starting to reduce. By forty-five she has the child-bearing capacity of, medically speaking, a paving slab.

At the same time the risks associated with pregnancy are on their way up. Down's Syndrome is the most common risk: just one in two thousand at age twenty, before rising sharply above the age of forty and peaking at one in twelve at forty-nine.

Us blokes are luckier. We can merrily keep our end of bargain until we croak. Look at Jack Nicholson, Clint Eastwood and Tony Curtis, they were all well on in life when they had kids. Curtis had been technically dead for three years.

Okay, there is some evidence that sperm from a man over the age of forty-one is slightly more likely to produce a Down's Syndrome baby. But the research was limited and inconclusive and, worst of all, was carried out by Belgians, so can probably be discounted.

You protest that if you wanted to be selfish (and let's face it, you normally do), why should a young spring chicken like you get involved in baby-making now? The thing to remember about Eastwood, Nicholson *et al*, is they are all handsome, multimillionaire movie stars who've snared young fertile beauties into their dotage. You, on the other hand, have the sex appeal of a jug-eared spot-welder from Harrogate. By the time you reach sixty-five the best thing you can hope to snare is a prolapsed spleen.

Seriously, there are advantages to becoming a dad in your twenties and thirties. You'll be young enough and fit enough to play with them. You are also probably entering your highest earning years.

Gross Domestic Products

You've read somewhere that just feeding and clothing a child up to the age of eighteen can cost £90,000. You could buy a small flat in Islington for that, a whole street in the arse-end of Cardiff. This is perfectly true but, unlike a *Reader's Digest* prize, you cannot reject the baby-prize and take the cash alternative. If you don't spend the money on bringing up a child you'll only fritter it away down the bookies or collecting rare back issues of *What Car?* magazine.

Having said that, fathering a baby has major financial implications. For example, your partner may want to give up work temporarily or completely. Rather than two people living on two incomes, there'll be three living on one income. At the same time you may reckon you need to move to a bigger house. If you're really lucky, the birth could coincide with a fifty grand fine for tax evasion. In short, having a baby could make a total mess of your financial stability.

Since when did you care? You're the bloke who spends two grand a year insuring a seven-year-old BMW. Last year the local publican added a conservatory to the back of the pub purely on the cash you put over the bar. But all of a sudden you're a cross between Ebenezer Scrooge and the Chancellor of the Exchequer. The plain truth is you're perfectly capable of buggering up your finances without the aid of a new family.

Bodily Functions

You know the facts of life inside out. You certainly don't need me to tell you how to get a woman pregnant. You've read thousands of magazine articles about it, all of them fully illustrated, and studied several meticulously detailed videos from places as far afield as Sweden and Germany.

But, on examining your credentials a little closer, you realise that your expertise is not so much biology as bonkology.

Which is surprising because biology was something you did study at school. You may remember homework spent tracing diagrams of Fallopian tubes from the textbook and plagiarising whole chunks of *Encyclopaedia Britannica*. But, when it comes down to it, how much of this Education, Education, Education actually stuck? It might be wise to remind you of some of the finer points of impregnating a woman.

Fertile Grounding

Infertility is a common problem. But one that so often comes as a shock. Countless times your dad warned you to be careful you didn't get someone pregnant. Normally this was done through the issuing of vague admonitions along the lines of, 'Look son, if you can't be good, be careful.' Or, 'Make sure you ruin the moment just before penetration by hunting through your jeans for a condom.'

My own father spelled out the full facts of life as he saw them to:

One up the bum, no harm done.

One up the fanny and your mum's a granny.

One in the breasts is as good as it gets.

One in the armpit, to see if she sweats.

Then came AIDS and even that advice fell down. Now not only did we have to worry about getting a girl into trouble but also had to avoid contracting some terrible disease. We were strapping on so much rubber we required a diving mask and snorkel.

Now at a time in our lives when we positively want to get a girl into trouble, we find it isn't that easy. The true chances of impregnating a woman on a one-night stand are actually fairly remote. But if this secret ever got out it would be the death of soap operas worldwide. Most of the cast of *EastEnders* would never have been born.

Research shows if a hundred people try for a baby for a whole year, by the end seventy-five per cent will have achieved pregnancy. For some it will take another year. But as many as ten per cent of couples will struggle for much longer to conceive. (If you met your wife in Brazil, it's worth investigating if you are unwittingly sharing your life with someone who's had a sex-change operation.)

Barren Knights

A lot of couples feel guilty if they are struggling to make a baby. Some find it hard to discuss the problem. Some more struggle to even confront there might be a problem. The important thing here is not to feel like anyone's failing. Apportioning blame won't get you anywhere. You need to examine causes. In very simple terms, these come in three categories: her fault, your fault and both your faults.

Her fault: normally this means problems with her ovulation or blocked Fallopian tubes. Simply put: either the eggs are not popping out of her ovaries every month, or, if they are, the chute they roll down to the womb is clogged up. (Every woman starts off with about half a million eggs inside her. They are there from the day she is born.)

Your fault: you suffer from low sperm count and too many malformed sperm. Every attempt to impregnate is akin to crossing no-man's land in the Battle of the Somme. Low sperm count means not enough troops coming out of the bunker. Malformed sperms mean plenty of troops but they are poorly trained and too badly equipped.

Both your faults: you are both on the borderline of conception capability and each of you could probably conceive with a more fertile partner.

The Sperm Accountant

You think to yourself, fine, let's see where the problem lies. You're big enough to admit it if it's your fault. In fact you are willing not just to count your sperm, but if necessary to investigate exactly who in the Gonad Department is responsible for this shortfall. You've always wondered about that left testicle of yours; something of an attitude problem. It's smaller and more misshapen than the right one and, now you come to think of it, the bastard thing refused to drop until you were fifteen.

Unfortunately, you can't count your own sperm. You have to go to the doctor and produce a sample.

Yes, that means what you think it does. Those fully illustrated magazine articles do come in useful after all. You are required to masturbate into a suitable receptacle. (An old yoghurt pot will suffice, but it should be clearly labelled before returning to the fridge.) Then take the sample to the clinic within a couple of hours. After analysis the doctor can tell you if you are producing enough.

To cover your embarrassment as you hand your doctor your still-warm sample, you inquire: 'So, doc, how many sperm do I need? A dozen, with maybe half a dozen Duncan Goodhews amongst them?'

'No,' he replies, 'a normal sperm count is around three hundred million in every ejaculation. With maybe seventy-five million strong swimmers. Of those probably less than fifty sperm make the journey all the way up the womb to the ovum. Just one sperm will pierce the egg.'

Every sperm that manages to find the ovum and join with it to make a baby is about six times as lucky as a lottery winner.

Counting Up, Cutting Down

You go back in a couple of days for the results. You're convinced there won't be a problem. You know whatever happens, wherever the problem lies, it'll be nobody's fault. But surely, please God, don't let it be yours.

The doctor greets you with a smile, a good sign. He seems cheerful, another good sign. He asks you to sit down. A bad sign, but maybe he's just being polite. He shuffles a few papers, clears his throat then blurts out, 'I'm afraid we may have to do further tests.'

You glance down at your left testicle thinking, 'I knew you were shooting blanks, you ugly curly-haired git.'

When you've calmed down a bit you ask the doctor if there's anything you can do to up your sperm count. He says yes, you can. That's the good news. The bad news is, he wants you to give up smoking.

He quotes Lord Robert Winston, the eminent fertility specialist (glasses, big moustache, did that TV show *The Human Body*). Winston says if you have a low sperm count and smoke more than eight fags per day, cut down. Better still, give up.

Right, then. Anything else? The doctor nods. But again the news is bad. He wants you to lose weight. Winston again: he cites a case (Infertility: A Sympathetic Approach) of a lorry driver who smoked forty a day and was three stone overweight. He cut his smoking down to four a day and lost weight by going to the gym. His wife became pregnant within five weeks. They had been trying for a baby for seven years.

This doctor is starting to wind you up. How can anybody give up smoking and lose weight at the same time? You decide to question him in a more pro-active manner. 'I don't suppose I

17

could circumvent all this by just boozing a bit more? I'm sure I could manage that. I could even switch to spirits if that would help.'

The doctor chuckles in a supercilious way that makes you want to punch him. No such luck. Winston recommends no more than three pints a day of beer or half a bottle of wine. Spirits, since you mention them, are the worst thing for a low sperm count.

Marijuana, cocaine, and even some prescription medications are thought to severely cut sperm count too. Unfortunately it's a case of sex *or* drugs and rock 'n' roll.

There is a common myth that wearing tight trousers can make you infertile, which is plainly ridiculous . . . but turns out to be true.

Testicles, like bottles of weak Mexican beer, are best served cool. Sperm production is enhanced when they are kept a few degrees below body temperature. To facilitate this, God invented the scrotum. (He didn't win too many design awards that year, but it seems to do the job.) Because of this some specialists advise against wearing *Saturday Night Fever* style, goods-in-the-window-where-all-the-chicks-can-see-them strides. They also suggest boxer shorts rather than Y-fronts. Very hot baths and saunas can be a problem too, particularly if your partner catches you coming out of one called Randy Rosie's Rub and Tug Parlour.

A more likely source of infertility in men is the presence of varicose veins around the testicles, known as 'variocele'. These can be corrected by a surgeon. Do not try it yourself at home, even if you own one of the really fancy Swiss Army knives.

First Rule of Sex

You have always suspected a link between sex and comedy, something to do with the chuckles when you strip down to your birthday suit. But both rely heavily on timing. If you want to get your partner pregnant, timing is everything.

Once every twenty-eight days a woman menstruates. During menstruation, lasting four or five days, she not only bleeds from the vagina but also dances around on roller skates wearing tight white trousers just to make sure her sanitary towel is performing correctly.

This period is not a time when fornication can result in conception. Well, thank heavens, God got something right.

Conception is most likely to take place around ovulation. This is between the eight and twelve days after the period has finished. However, sperm can live in the vagina for up to four days, so any intercourse that takes place from the fourth day could still be alive to fertilise her ovum. Between the thirteenth day and her next menstruation a woman is said to be infertile.

If all this sounds complicated, don't worry, it is. It is also the basis of the rhythm method of contraception practised by devout Catholics. That's why they all end up with fifteen kids.

XYZ of Selection

You wonder what sex your child will be. You wonder if there's anything you can do to affect the sex. One popular theory contends if you have sex in the morning rather than the evening you are more likely to get a boy. Not true, but it does make the commute into work seem somehow less arduous.

One possible way to influence the sex of your baby is when in relation to ovulation you have sex. Boy sperm, known as X sperm, are fast swimmers, but have little stamina. Girl sperm, Y sperm, swim slower, but last longer.

Sperm that arrives early in womb will have to hang around waiting for the egg to drop. In this case, the 'long-life' girl sperm have a better chance of piercing the egg. Conversely, if the egg is already in position when the sperm goes in, the fast-swimming boy sperms have the best chance of winning. In conclusion, early cycle sex is more likely to produce girls and late cycle sex would make more boys.

For all sorts of reasons this technique is in no way foolproof. Even if you are successful in achieving a particular sex, the gods may decide to play a trick on you in the same way as they did Mr and Mrs Clary or Mr and Mrs Widdecombe.

2
First Three Months: Blooming and Barfing

Interference On Picture

You come home from work one night and your partner has some news for you. It's important news, she says. You better come in the living room and sit down.

But hold up a second, you have some important news of your own. The pub up the High Road is doing draft Guinness at £1 a pint all evening tonight. They also have Sky TV who are broadcasting the vital second leg of the Auto Windshields Cup. You're meeting your best mate Alan there in twenty minutes so, if there's no dinner made, you'll grab a Kentucky on the way up.

With this you head for the bedroom to get changed. You get halfway when she blurts out, 'I think I'm pregnant.'

You freeze. You give your head a little shake, relax, then take another step. You freeze again.

She thinks she's pregnant. She thinks your whole lives are about to be turned upside down. She thinks your two carefree spirits are henceforth going to be bound inexorably till your dying days by this miraculous coalescence of your gene pools.

All of this rocks you. But what you're really thinking is, does this mean I can't go to the pub? Further consideration delivers the body blow that you probably won't even make it for the second half.

She Thinks, Therefore She Might Be

From somewhere you dredge up a smile and turn to your partner. She looks all of a sudden very beautiful in a frail, vulnerable way. Her eyes are wide; her mouth quivers on the edge of several competing emotions.

As the true significance of the moment dawns on you, you bring yourself rapidly to your senses. We're talking about parenthood here. Who cares about another night with stupid tight-fisted Alan watching some crappy Cup game only complete anoraks consider important? Missing the half-price Guinness will hurt for a long time, but as the months and years go on the pain will diminish and, eventually, seem almost silly. Come, come, there'll be other promotions.

You question her a little closer. She thinks she's pregnant. Could this be merely a scare? But her period is a week late. She's very regular. She thinks she must be pregnant. Again the word 'thinks' is used. Hasn't she had a look? Or a feel . . . whatever? Done a test, that's it. No, she wanted you to be there when she did the test. She wants you two to do the test together.

What the hell for? Why put you through the agonies and anxieties of expectation when she could easily have shouldered them alone?

She suggests you nip up to the late-night chemist in the High Road for a pregnancy-testing kit. You agree readily. A little too readily. She glances at the clock and entreats you to come *straight* back. Oh please, surely she gives you some credit.

She apologises, and that apology is still ringing in your ears as you gulp down your half-price Guinness and catch the first five minutes. You explain to Alan you'll have to go because your partner might be pregnant. Alan says that's brilliant news, no need to buy you a pint back then.

Entering the pharmacy you notice the chemist watching you as you peruse the shelves for a kit. The smile on his face suggests he knows something's afoot. Then you get the second big shock of the day: the pregnancy testing kit costs £11.99. Ouch! No wonder the chemist is smiling. By the time you've bought a packet of Smints for your breath this ten-minute outing will have cost you nearly twenty quid. You'd heard that having children was an expensive business.

Pregnancy-testing kits all work on the same principle, by measuring the amount of hCG (human Chorionic Gonadotrophin) in a woman's urine. This hormone is released by the fertilised egg from fourteen days after conception (i.e. if you remember, conception takes place halfway through a cycle, so by the time the next (missed) period is reached, fourteen days should have elapsed).

Shelling out twelve quid seemed pretty offensive and the prospect of sloshing about with buckets of your partner's pee is hardly solace. But actually the process is pretty straightforward and apparently 90 per cent accurate.

The hardest part is finding a clean jar in which to collect the sample. Avoid using a jar half full of white spirit with a paint brush sticking out of the top, as this may contaminate the urine sample. To combat this, remove the white spirit before attempting to collect the sample. At the very least, remove the paint brush. It may cause injury.

Once collected, a few drops of the sample are then poured into the testing capsule. If the test is positive the sample changes

"Apparently if I'm pregnant, you turn white!"

colour. Some testing capsules produce a ring. If you're un-married, you might find yourself under pressure to react like-wise.

A variety of alternative testing methods are available, including the popular 'pee on a lolly stick' variety which saves on the jar collecting bit.

This is the news that will change your lives for ever. She's going to be a mum and you're going to be a dad. She is pregnant. And you, in a way, are pregnant too!

If you are too tight to pay for a home kit, there is another reli-able method that's completely free. You merely wait nine months then check to see if there are three plates laid out at breakfast each morning.

Whichever way you go, your partner will be required to go to the doctor's who may ask her to take a further test. Exactly the same hormone is measured as with the home kit but it's more accurate and makes the doctor feel useful. (Normally this is free but some surgeries charge.) The doctor will then count forward forty weeks (from the date of her last period) to give your deliv-ery date.

Pop Your Cork

You'll want to celebrate the news and be in no doubt the arrangement of this (and any subsequent) celebration is very much your territory. It's no good protesting that she never arranged anything either. It's down to you.

Don't complain. Rather, enjoy and savour these interludes when you can be useful. They are few and far between. Whereas your partner will stay indispensable right up to and beyond the delivery of the baby, you peaked during the quarter minute it took you to ejaculate. Metaphorically speaking, conception may have been the beginning of a long, round-the-world style journey for her, but you were merely dropping her at the airport. Actually that's too generous; in the scheme of things you were about as important as the bloke who clipped her ticket on the Gatwick Express.

Congratulations can be achieved in several ways. For example, presenting a dozen red roses is a cliché, but such a romantic ges-ture that she will certainly be overjoyed. They have the added virtue of being available at the traffic lights on the North Circular for three quid. A box of chocolates produces the same effect, but unfortunately this will often require a detour to the shops, finding a place to park, getting out of the car, etc. etc. . . . then agonising for twenty minutes as to whether the small £3.99 box is suitably impressive or if you have to take the next step up to the £14.99 four-layer, fat-git special.

If I may offer a personal recommendation, make a reservation at your local bijou eatery whence you can whisk your partner directly from the doctor's surgery. This is an important day, a private moment of festival for the two of you before you unleash the news on the world. Push the boat out and have a lovely meal together. Better still, order a really fine bottle of wine from the à la carte menu safe in the knowledge that now she's pregnant you'll get to drink the entire lot by yourself.

Worst Kept Secret

As you return from the restaurant you discuss the protocol of who to tell and when. Your mother should be first because she's desperate for grandchildren . . . but no, her mother should be first, the mother of the mother and all that . . . or rather it should be her sister, they've always been close . . . The simplest solution would be to get them all round for tea and tell them all at once. Unfortunately, the two sets of parents do not get on. They don't exactly hate each other, but your mum thinks her dad is a drunk and her mum suspects your dad could well be the guy who burgled their house last Christmas.

You toy with the idea of keeping the news secret. Retain it just between the two of you for a few weeks or so. This appeals to the devil in you. Pretend she's just putting on a bit of weight. (Very believable; she's always liked her food.) Then, the first they know about it is when you bring around a fully formed three-year-old who greets them with, 'Morning, Gran. Now we meet I can see how I ended up with this enormous hooter.'

Arriving back at your flat, you are still discussing who should have the privilege of this info, when you bump into the greasy-haired dispatch rider who lives in the top flat. Despite the fact that you hardly know him and secretly wish he would move, you blurt out the news. This is the man who parks his Norton Commando in the hall and has a penchant for 2 a.m. sing-a-longs with Kurt Cobain. He becomes the first to know.

You have discovered that this news doesn't respect any protocol. It is too momentous. These are beans that demand to be spilled.

Dirty Little Secret Hope

Now the secret is out, you do the rounds talking about your forthcoming event until your face is bluer than a royal tampon. One particular question is asked again and again. What do you want, a girl or a boy? Be aware this is a loaded question. Your partner will be watching to see how you reply.

You know in your heart of hearts you don't mind if it's a girl or a boy. You have no preference. You just secretly hope to hell it's a boy. If it's a girl it won't be a total disaster. You won't mind. You won't disown her. You'll love her just as much. You just can't imagine being a father to a girl. Which is natural. When you were a baby you were a boy yourself. You experienced the whole of childhood as a male (trying on your mum's underwear notwithstanding). Your formative relationships were that of a son: mother-son; father-son; on-me-head-son.

As formerly established, you know complete zilch about babies. It's fair to say you know even less about baby girls.

Your dirty little secret hope is nothing to worry about. Hope away to your heart's content. Just make sure you keep it secret. Don't let on to your partner. She won't and can't understand this feeling. Deep down she probably wants a girl just as much as you want a boy and for all the same reasons. Her feelings may be confused by the fact that she wants desperately to please you. Because despite the fact that you've kept your secret tightly under lock and key, she *knows* you want a boy. (This is no excuse to reveal the secret.)

When you get asked the boy or girl question, reply, flat-faced, toothy-grinned: 'I don't mind, as long as it's healthy.'

Don't assume everyone knows you're lying. Don't try to get flash – 'I want a girl, because I want her to play for England and score the winning goal in the World Cup Final of . . . that is the, er, Netball World Cup final.'

Behind your secret hope is the desire to have someone to be blokish with when they're grown up. Relax: these days a lot of girls are more blokish than blokes. They drink pints, swear like troopers and chase around for one-night stands. If you want to increase the odds of this behaviour you could always move to Manchester. Okay, the chances of your daughter playing in the Premiership are fairly slim, but if your son shows the same kind of poise and ball control you possess neither will he.

Beans, Beans, Good For Your Belly

Your partner has something growing inside her. What started off as a tiny bundle of cells will, through the miracle of nature, grow into a great big bundle of cells.

The embryo will go from an infinitesimal speck at conception to something the size of a baked bean at six weeks. It also looks a bit like a baked bean, half folded over in the middle. The embryo also has black dots at the top which are the eyes and tiny flipper-like protrusions which will form the hands and feet. Baked beans have none of these traits unless you are so poor you have to buy one of the supermarket 'value' brands.

By three months the embryo has enlarged to the size of a Spanish onion. The fingers and toes are already becoming visible. The kidneys produce urine. Preferences for a political party are already being formed, but views on proportional representation are still a little muddy.

Warning: some couples are initially disturbed by the thought of a living thing growing inside them. If so, avoid renting any of the *Alien* trilogy until the phase passes.

Return of the Big Mac

One of the early symptoms of pregnancy is feelings of severe nausea or actual vomiting upon waking. The simplest cure is to avoid getting so sloshed the night before. You won't just feel better but will be able to assist your partner with her morning sickness.

Alternatively, have a second toilet bowl fitted beside the first one to avoid congestion in the bathroom.

Your partner's nausea is caused by increased hormone levels given off by the placenta and a reduced blood-sugar level. To combat this, she may ask you to fetch her a cup of sweet tea before she rises from bed. No change there, then. She may ask for a couple of biscuits, some lightly buttered toast, some cornflakes with a little skimmed milk and topped with raisins. You may suggest she wants to cut out the middle man and start sleeping in the larder.

Some of the things that induce morning sickness are the cooking smells of fatty foods, alcohol and coffee. This probably sounds like a tremendous breakfast hangover cure to you, but will more than likely make her throw up.

Many experts believe morning sickness is psychological, possibly even ritualistic: a woman's way of convincing herself she is truly pregnant. Anthropologists report that in some cultures women never experience morning sickness. Instead they suffer from boils or have vivid fertility dreams of themselves becoming a ripe fruit exploding with seeds. So maybe you got off lightly. Fetching the odd biscuit must be better than sleeping with a boil-ridden hag who every night turns into a nine-stone kumquat.

The Scargill Diet

In early pregnancy many women experience strange food cravings. These range from the slightly abnormal to the darn-right bonkers.

Under the slightly abnormal column will fall such things as smoked fish and custard or gherkins with ice cream. Under bonkers we have things like pot noodle and spam.

Some women even suffer from a condition known as 'pica'. A subconscious desire to obtain more iron in their diet leads them to crave substances such as soil and even coal.

You may find such uncontrollable urges in your partner alarming. No need. Coal may contain little in the way of vitamins and protein but is extremely high in fibre. And what better thing to warm you up on a chilly winter's afternoon than a lump of coal. In summer, why not get a few other pregnant mums around and have a barbecue in the garden. So economical, there's no need to buy any food at all. (Note: government regulations state pregnant women in built-up areas should consume only a smokeless fuel.)

You may have heard the expression eating for two. This is a dangerous myth that can lead to permanent weight gain. In reality she is using her pregnancy to be extremely greedy. Shake her by the shoulders and demand: 'Get a grip, lady. Pregnant or not, that nosebag was designed for a horse.'

During pregnancy the tendency to over-eat is compounded by heightened cravings for fatty foods or sweets. But don't over-react, the odd bar of chocolate or bag of chips will hurt neither her nor the baby. Nor is a flame-grilled cheeseburger oozing with ketchup and mayonnaise the end of world. A joint of battered lard, served on a bed of Camembert and drenched in WD40, should be restricted to an occasional treat.

Alien Nation

The new responsibility you feel for your partner and your

upcoming baby has altered your perspective on life. The world actually looks different.

Driving to work, your sharpened view reveals an alien culture inhabiting the streets. Mums pushing prams along, dads dropping their kids off at school; where did these characters come from? You knew these 'parents' existed but you hadn't realised they were around in such numbers.

You drive past a billboard advertising baby food. You've never seen that before. Switching on the radio you catch a news item on nursery-school funding, a discussion on dangerous toys. So this alien culture has its own programming?

Entering your office, you are astounded to discover a huge branch of Mothercare right next door. Where on earth did that spring from? It certainly wasn't there yesterday.

A Couple of Swingers

Pregnancy is an exciting time. Life is full of renewed purpose. Suddenly you both feel very grown up. She may be sick as a parrot but you two are certainly over the moon.

Her moods can swing the other way too as the hormones invading her body make her irritable. An ordinary discussion between the pair of you can spiral into a prolonged and bitter argument. The main thing is to be watchful for trouble brewing. Take a few breaths then begin nodding and smiling, and keep doing so no matter how cock-eyed your partner's position appears. Then, in low monotone, repeat every few seconds, 'Yes, darling, of course, darling. You're so right, darling. Of course, darling.' To preserve self-respect think of these words as merely a calming mantra with absolutely no bearing on the real world.

Even this approach can occasionally excite even more vicious dispute. Your partner may accuse you of being a patronising bastard with ugly fat love-handles and a hooked nose. If you think such escalation is likely, a simple padlock can be attached to secure a cutlery drawer. Plastic dinner services, of the type employed for a summer picnic, are largely unbreakable. An old suit jacket worn back-to-front and secured with strong tape will suffice as a straitjacket.

Moody Old You

Men get moody, too, during early pregnancy. Unfortunately, you can't blame it on an extra gallon or two of hormones washing through your system. So what causes this?

You might think it's all the fetching and carrying you are having to do for your sickly partner. You might think it's because she's winding you up summink rotten with all these rows. The chances are though it is caused by stress. Stress brought on by thoughts of responsibility and change.

You realise that, in a few short months, you will have to become responsible, sensible and set a good example like dads are supposed to. Within a year you will have to become a stickler for table manners, correct speaking, and putting filthy underwear in the hamper. You recall your own father's Victorian values.

Your memory is playing tricks with you. Dads occasionally spout off about such things but only when they are irritable. Most of the time they behave not merely as badly as the kids, but as badly as the naughtiest kid you know. This is their true role. If you wanted to put on your best trousers then have a mud fight in the garden that was fine as long as you could get Dad involved. If you accidentally said the 'F' word in front of your mum, your cast-iron excuse was, 'Dad says it sometimes. Dad says it all the time when he's drunk.'

Fatherly responsibilities that will have to be faced are things like reading the Sunday papers at interminable length, snoring on the couch after dinner and humming the tunes to adverts whilst driving. Most of these are achievable in a few years with very little conscious effort.

One of the joys of entering family life second time around is seeing everything from a different perspective. It's like being in a play you know well, but playing a different role. This time you get to be the lazy irascible old codger who gets to boss everyone around.

Miscarriage

Miscarriage is shockingly common. It is estimated that up to twenty per cent of first pregnancies miscarry. Many of these are due to the embryo not evolving correctly and would lead to a seriously deformed foetus. The riskiest time for miscarriage is between the eleventh and thirteenth week of pregnancy. (For this reason, some people like to delay spreading the news of pregnancy too widely until after this time.)

Your partner will certainly be upset. You will be also. But it

can be hard for men to understand the depth of grief their partner feels. You couldn't feel the pregnancy, or see any outward
sign of it.

Your natural reaction to miscarriage might be to make yourself scarce and hope all this heavy stuff goes away quickly.
However, your partner's coming to terms with it may be helped
by both discussing your feelings. Give her plenty of time to get
back to normal and then try for another baby. A single miscarriage does not mean there is any increased likelihood of
miscarrying again.

Do You Copy?

Your partner comes off the phone from talking to her mother
looking pleased with herself. Oh yeah, you think, what have that
lot cooked up this time? You bide your time before plunging in
and asking. You bide for at least ninety seconds, then . . .

'Come on, out with it,' you say.

'Out with what?'

'We're absolutely not going down to their cottage for Bank
Holiday weekend. I'm playing golf with Alan on Sunday and I'm
spending Monday in the pub. The whole of Monday. As agreed.
Weeks ago. And anyway their spare room stinks of old people.'

'So what am I supposed to do?'

'You can caddy, I've always said that. When we first went out
you used to caddy.'

'I am pregnant, in case you've forgotten.'

'Oh, right. You're worried your dawdling might hold up play
for the members.'

'Sod the members.'

'Dead right. Stuck-up gits. Tell you what, do nine holes and
we'll review the situation.'

You are not a monster. You know you are being slightly
unreasonable, but you thought if you could damp down
expectations she might decide to go to her parents' alone that
weekend. She might as well – Saturday you're going to an all-day
pool competition.

Later that night, it transpires you were barking up the wrong
tree. She rolls over in bed and announces:

'Mum and I were discussing names. What do you think of
Xavier?'

'Bloody good photocopiers. What names did you come up
with?'

'Xavier is the name. What do you think?'

'I think it's disgusting. Is there someone who doesn't?'

'Yes, me and Mum. It's a Spanish name.'

'Well, let some Spanish kid have it then. It probably means squid pie swimming in olive oil and garlic. No kid of mine is being called Xavier. No way, José.'

'I quite like José.'

'All right then, no way, bollock breath.'

Choosing names can be a source of argument during pregnancy. But normally the discussions are a lot of fun. You discover every single normal name has a connotation of some sort.

Harry will always be associated with your Uncle Harry, who has a squint and stutters. Jack is popular but reminds everyone of cousin Jack who's serving seven years for armed robbery. Susan is a tall slender name but your Great Aunt Sue is four foot three and weighs seventeen stone.

Richard, William or Robert would not seem to pose any problems but, on second examination, could easily become Dick, Willy or Nobby. You both like Michael but that will become either 'Mick' which is awful or 'Mike' which doesn't fare too well with surnames such as Hockey, Hunt or Rapper-Needs-Cleaning.

Girls' names are no better. Any Jane will always be accused of being plain. Ludmilla is a pretty name but sounds like a shot-putter. All Gertrudes, Constances and Bridgits will be doomed to spinsterdom, whereas Vickys, Pamelas and Morags will undoubtedly end up on the game.

Even when you do choose a name it may develop connotations unforeseen. Plenty of well-to-do people probably chose the gung-ho, outdoorsy name of Forrest. Then came the film *Forrest Gump*. Boy, did he love school that summer. Another couple had a daughter a year or so back. They christened her 'Monica', a sister for young Bill.

Even in these enlightened days not too many parents will want to pigeon hole a child with names such at Les-lie, or Gay-lord, or even By-ron. But once you go down that road you begin to rule out names like Sadie and Dominic.

On the positive side, you can have names that reflect your interests. Portia and Mercedes are perfectly acceptable girls' names along with Austen and Ford for the twin boys. They go particularly well with surnames such as Jordan, Maclaren Williams and even the Germanic name of Van Transit.

Chelsea fans have an obvious eponymous offering. Arsenal

supporters must look beyond, but first names such as Arsene and Dennis don't help much. What about combining a couple of names, although Dixon-Seaman hardly suggests a clean sheet, and Nwankwo-Parlour could find his name above a shop in Soho.

3

Second Three Months: Scans, Plans and Automobiles

The Test Was Rigged

Your partner claims to be thirteen weeks pregnant, but you're beginning to wonder. Okay, she's spent the last three months singing into the big white telephone every morning. In the meantime you've done more housework than you have in your entire life. You've put pillows under feet, chocolate biscuits beside cups of tea, even provided extra lumps of coal for her cornflakes. A question crosses your mind.

'Where's the bump?'

Nothing shows at all. Not that you can see. Believe me, you've looked. She's still wearing the same jeans she always did. Button is sometimes undone, but only after a big meal. She was fatter than this when she came back from that week visiting her mate in Stevenage. Could it be that she's not really pregnant at all? And the last three months have been a cunning ruse to get you charging around like a blue-arsed fly doing her beck and call twenty-four hours a day.

Not exactly a question you can drop into conversation. But the doubts remain.

However, these doubts are unfounded. She is pregnant. The fact

33

is, her tummy bump doesn't grow so it shows until about twenty weeks. Yes, five months. And she won't be really blimping up in any kind of impressive manner until more like thirty weeks.

So get the rubber gloves on, and the pinafore, stick the handle of the squeegee mop up your rear-end and get on with the house-work.

New Improved Formula

From now on, though, things will start to look up. Your partner will start to feel better. Whereas in the first twelve weeks she did not look pregnant but acted it, in the next three months she will start to look pregnant but become invigorated.

It is during this time that some women begin to bloom. Cheeks look rosier and plumper, smoothing out any lines. This is because extra blood is being pumped to her skin. Pregnancy also increases the rate of growth of hair. It looks better, thicker and shinier. She's virtually turning into a breakfast TV anchorwoman.

Her moods have improved too. She is less irritable, probably because she has her energy back. From about sixteen weeks her foetus-induced hangovers will settle down. No more staggering back from the toilet in the mornings looking like a heroin addict.

If your partner is in a full-time job she will have found it a real struggle up to now. Colleagues at work have been less than com-pletely sympathetic. Probably because they too may have been thinking, 'Oh yeah? So where's the bump?'

Of course, not every woman blooms. The increased bodily secretions can make their hair more oily and lank. She complains her feet get sweaty. Spots seem to be breaking out on her face. She's suddenly going through the teenage uglies again.

But you don't mention anything. Her hair may be a bit greasy but it's certainly thicker. Unfortunately, the condition has spread to her body hair. And that hair seems to have gone darker. Crikey, she's got more hair than the neighbour's dog.

Once again you don't mention it. Neither do you offer to change the fuse on her Lady Shave.

The most important thing to remember, it's a temporary thing. Most women look better, a few look worse. The phase will pass.

Closer to Jeremy

So her moods have improved. Her energy has come back and normality is restored. Once again you're happily ensconced in front of the goggle box watching *Top Gear* as she plies you with toasted sandwiches and mugs of tea.

Jeremy Clarkson is testing a new flashy off-roader. You suggest the vehicle might just fit the bill what with a bairn on the way. She agrees and sits down to take a closer look. You cuddle on the sofa and dream of your future . . . motoring holidays through the Lake District in your big chunky four-wheeler . . . little junior on the rear seat cooing happily . . . perhaps a newly acquired family mutt yapping excitedly at the back.

You slide along the sofa for a cuddle. She feels soft and warm. She's happy and relaxed. Maybe this pregnancy lark isn't so bad after all.

Three In a bed (and the Little One Said . . .)

The on-rush of bodily fluids that made her bloom has made her libido come back too. The increased blood supply making her shiny on the outside is also working on the inside.

So sex is firmly back on the agenda, but you have some worries that intercourse may be a risk to the foetus. It is not. If it feels comfortable and enjoyable for her (we know it feels as good as ever to you) then it is perfectly safe. There's no need to worry that your unborn child is being pummelled. Neither is the poor thing desperately dodging and weaving around the womb trying to avoid a knock-out punch.

Your partner may prefer a position which means less pressure on her tummy or less deep penetration. If intercourse is not preferred, as an alternative, oral sex is completely safe. (Although suggesting it may not be.)

What's really different about your sex life now is how you feel about each other. The closeness you felt dreaming about that new off-roader has spilled into the bedroom. Your love-making is calmer and richer, full of love and understanding. It also comes with free servicing and six-year anti-corrosion guarantee.

The Good News Just Got Better

And while we're making positive points, here's a couple more you may already be aware of. During pregnancy women's boobs get bigger. They're fuller, firmer and stickier-outer. This is due to production of something called colostrum in the ducts of the mammary glands. A few days after the baby is born this colostrum will turn into milk.

Your partner may leak a little of this creamy substance from the nipple during love-making. If you accidentally swallow some, there's nothing to worry about and no need to contact the emergency services. It contains mostly protein and is low fat and low sugar, so could actually aid slimming (but only when used in conjunction with a calorie-controlled diet).

Tickets, Please

From the second three months onwards you will begin to realise being pregnant is seen as a 'medical condition'. Like any medical condition this means tests, scans and examinations by a variety of doctors, nurses, consultants etc. They call it ante-natal care.

It's true to say some people yearn for the days when attitudes were more cold-blooded. At the turn of the century a woman would merely squat down, pull her knickers to one side, give a couple of short snorts and produce a gurgling child. Obviously this is a slightly rose-tinted view, but even today you could imagine someone like Sarah Ferguson or Germaine Greer carrying it off with such minimal fuss. Fergie might not even have to squat, just lengthen her stride a bit.

'Haw, haw, haw, isn't childbirth such jolly fun? Just the thing before a game of polo, what!'

The upside of ante-natal care is that childbirth is safer than ever in history. The downside is regular hospital visits and trips to ante-natal clinics. We all know what a drag it is hanging around for hours on end in hospital waiting areas.

Your partner suggests your active role in this pregnancy should include keeping her company. Being a regular guy you agree to go along. You put up with a long waiting-room stint only to find that you don't even get to enter the examination room. It's like queuing to get into Wimbledon and then being told you can't go into Centre Court. (Which is exactly what does happen at Wimbledon. After a three-day queue in the pouring rain you get the privilege of standing beside Court 117 to watch a quartet of Uruguayan over-fifties play mixed-doubles.)

Next time she asks, you are ready. You say you don't want to hog *all* the joy of participation. That would be selfish. Why not allow someone else a turn? A friend, perhaps? Or her mother, or your mother, or, er . . . anybody actually. What about that gossipy old bag who runs the launderette, if she's so bloody interested?

Finding yourself in the hot seat again you take some advice

from a pregnancy magazine which suggests approaching a hospital visit like a long train journey: take along some newspapers, a book, a Walkman, even Travel Scrabble to pass the time. The trouble is the way you normally get through a long train journey is to make a bee-line for the buffet car and neck down several tins of McEwan's Tartan, then totter off to the toilet cubicle for a long relaxing bowel movement.

Ultrasonic Bloom

A hospital visit you won't want to miss is when they do The Scan.

In fact The Scan is something you have been waiting for with bated breath. Mates down the pub, blokes who wouldn't know a pregnant woman if she sat on them, have been asking if you'd had The Scan yet.

(Actually there are normally two scans: an early scan at around five months' pregnancy and a late scan at thirty-four weeks. Nowadays some hospitals even offer a damned early scan at three months. If scans continue at this rate you'll hardly have time to roll off.)

You rightly see The Scan as the highlight of ante-natal care, like a Best Man's speech at a wedding or a first slug of lager on a hot day. It is the medical equivalent of the bit where Sharon Stone crosses her legs in *Basic Instinct*. Except in that scene no special technology was needed to get a good look at Miss Stone's insides.

Hospitals seem to realise this too. It's one examination where they don't treat you, the expectant father, as some kind of perverted interloper when you turn up with your partner. At The Scan they invite you to come right in, pull up a chair between the bed and the monitor screen and watch the action.

You anticipate seeing a video of little junior kicking about in his private aquarium. A movie trailer image sails across your mind:

Scan IV – The Foetus Kicks Back
Arnie Schwarzenegger IS the Consultant Paediatrician. Bruce Lee IS Kung Fu Foetus. Rest assured this film IS gratuitously violent.

As the radiologist readies equipment, you tip back in your chair. You are about to flip your shoes off and plant your stockinged feet on the edge of the bed when a dirty look from your partner snaps you back into reality.

You start to wonder what kind of picture quality you can expect. In what magnitude of detail will your unborn child be displayed? You vaguely remember seeing a still from the Sunday supplements: a foetus sucking its thumb. That scan was in pin-sharp focus and vibrant Technicolor, almost as though it was looking through a window right into the fleshy decompression chamber of your partner's tummy. Perhaps you can offer your nipper a thumbs up. 'Good luck on the way out, mate. We're all rooting for you out here.' He might even give you a wave back.

Your partner loosens her clothing. The nurse squelches some gel on to her tummy. It looks like hair gel but must be some kind of high-tech focusing solution. With exaggerated deliberateness the nurse gently lowers the scanning hardware down on to your partner's skin.

The excitement you both feel is almost too much bear. You give her hand a little squeeze. Ah, the wonders of modern science. How lucky you are to live in the Twenty-first Century.

Then . . .

Then . . . nothing.

'Er, miss, there seems to be something wrong with your telly.'

'No, no. It's fine.'

'But . . . but . . . I can't make out a thing.'

'Yes, you can. There's your baby there.'

Where? All you can see is a load of white noise.

'There it is, moving its legs about,' insists the radiologist pointing to the screen.

Certainly there is something, a vague something, moving around, but you'd never know it was a baby. It's more like underwater footage from the *Titanic*. You are beginning to fear disappointment with The Scan. You feel like you've just rented *Basic Instinct* only to discover the video version has Stone wearing baggy blue bloomers that come down to her knees.

Then you have an idea.

'Tell you what, miss, I'll twiddle the buttons on the telly while you move the aerial about at the back. See if between us we can make something out of this awful mess, eh?'

Eventually the radiologist explains that this is nothing like a movie at all. This is an Ultrasound Scan.

Ultrasound works by beaming high-frequency sound waves into the woman's stomach. This 'technology', if you can call it that, is the same one developed in World War II to locate submarines. You may remember how successful we were against the German U-boat. The technology is actually so basic even rum-sodden North-Sea trawlermen attempt to use it to find fish. Most of them are now so cod-less and skate-bereft they are going bankrupt.

You are perfectly at liberty to complain to the nurse that The Scan has failed to live up to its crack, but don't expect much joy. You see, the hospital might have invited you in, but have still missed the point. They see The Scan not primarily for the voyeuristic pleasure of the parents-to-be but as a medical test to reveal possible foetal abnormalities such as spina bifida and heart defects.

This is the whole problem with the Health Service: long queues, surly service and absolutely no mission to entertain. A bit of presentational advice from Disney might not go amiss.

(Those pictures in the Sunday supplements are done with a fetoscope, a type of endoscope. They were all the rage in the 1970s to detect birth defects. Fetoscopy may provide great pictures but is very dangerous to the foetus, with a high risk of miscarriage.)

Little Plonker

One thing you might find out is the sex of the child. But you will have to ask as the majority of people still don't want to know.

How does the radiologist do this? Obviously she is used to looking at fuzzy underwater pictures and may be able to make out whether the foetus is endowed with a tiny plonker, whereby it is unsurprisingly a boy. This may sound a fairly rudimentary way of telling the sex but when you think this willy is no more than a couple of millimetres long it takes some spotting even with the aid of the Ultrasound Scan. Nurses, the cruel ones, have been known to call for an Ultrasound machine after climbing into bed with a poorly endowed junior doctor.

Capricious Fancy

You decide you do want to know the sex of the baby. You figure it gets you out of the dirty-little-secret-hope conundrum once and for all. The hackneyed question down the pub, 'What do you want, a girl or a boy?' can be dealt with swiftly and honestly.

'Actually, we've had The Scan. We're having a girl. We're very pleased.'

Or alternatively, 'Get your Arsenal season tickets booked for 2020. My wife is about to present the world with the next Tony Adams.'

You are about to stand the pub a round of drinks when someone (a Spurs supporter) responds: 'You mean he'll drink fifteen pints before lunch time, wet the bed every night, and lollop about like an animal with its tail pinned on to the wrong place.'

Double Jeopardy

If you do decide to ask what sex the baby is, expect not one from two possible answers but one from four:

1 It looks like a boy.

2 A little girl, I think.

3 I don't know because I can't see its willy but I can tell you it will have a humungous pair of buttocks.

4 One of each.

One of each? Yes, you are having twins. The sixteen-week early scan is normally the first indication of twins, or triplets, or quins . . .

Imagine what it was like for that bloke in America whose wife had octuplets.

'Hit me with the news, doc, what we having?'

'Let's see now . . . A blonde, a brunette, three redheads, a couple of afros, and one poor little sod looks like he's as bald as a coot.'

Yikes. That guy must be getting a bill for nappies that would make Bill Gates gag on his milkshake.

Many blokes view the prospect of twins as both a financial and supervisional headache. It's true you have to stump up for two of everything; cots, high chairs, baby walkers. You will also have to help out changing two lots of nappies, feeding two mouths, bathing two babies. You suspect you'll be busy as a one-armed knife juggler with a gnat bite on his scrotum. But there are compensations.

Actually you are very lucky, particularly if the kids are different sexes. The luckiest, richest and tightest bloke I know had boy-girl non-identical twins. We all have a mate like this. The sort of bloke who gets on *Who Wants To Be a Millionaire*, then phones a friend, first making sure he can reverse the charges, then he gets a crossed line with Dr Stephen Hawking. The twins meant he had a ready-made family in one go. Done. Finished. Completemundo. His wife had only one pregnancy to go through, and was back in work for good within a year of giving birth.

Twins are extra aggro in the short term but in the long run they save time and money. The people to feel sorry for are the ones who already have kids, get accidentally pregnant again then discover they are expecting a multiple birth. That guy in America with the octuplets already had four kids.

Fruit of the Womb

As the middle three months of pregnancy arrive the foetus becomes recognisable as a baby, albeit a very ugly one.

At this stage the head is huge in comparison with the body, with large bulbous eyes that actually show through the translucent skin of its eyelids.

It gets worse. This pre-formed baby is also a wide-gobbed, chinless wonder that's covered in a type of fur called lanugo. Mr and Mrs William Hague would no doubt be delighted to produce a child with such stunning good looks. The rest of us can be grateful there is still plenty of development to go.

In the first trimester your baby progressed from a tiny egg to a small bean, then on to Spanish onion size. By four months it has progressed further, elongating into the dimensions of a large King Edward potato. Why not get these items out of the larder at home, line them up on the counter and witness the growth for yourself? Then mix all the ingredients in a bowl and fry for three minutes to enjoy a nourishing Spanish tortilla.

By five months the vegetable dimensions have thankfully been exhausted. But metaphor-buffs can still get their fix by knowing the baby is the size and length of a telephone hand set, complete with curly umbilical cord and, on the more expensive models, auto-redial and 0898 call-barring.

Drinking For Two

The much heralded scan may not quite have lived up to expectations but it did impress one thing very clearly. There really is a baby in there. In a few short months you really are going to be a real dad, really-really-really. In fact, by the time the six months are up, the foetus has a decent chance of survival even if it were to be born immediately.

Two things happen here inside your brain. Firstly, you are extremely happy and secondly, you are absolutely terrified. The burden of expectation could leave you feeling depressed.

You might not even realise you are depressed. Patterns of behaviour to look out for include hitting the bottle after work, getting home and slumping sullenly in front of the TV whilst refusing to converse with your spouse. Your spouse might not even realise you are depressed, as this is how you act most of the time anyway.

Emotional Morons

Eventually when the message filters down to your booze-befuddled brain that you are depressed, you don't have a clue either why or how to deal with it. By the time you realise you need to get in touch with your emotions, you discover they have changed their name and emigrated to a small otter farm in Siberia.

It's not your fault. *Cosmopolitan* might run quizzes on how to find the inner self but you rarely find them in *What Car?* Neither does *Total Football* run articles on 'Psychic Free Kicks: Hit a Banana Shot Around Your Wall Of Anxiety' or 'How To Cope When You're Mentally Three-Nil Down'.

Chances are the increasing reality of your situation has brought on a touch of Woolly Jumper Syndrome. You imagine yourself in a few months time spending every Friday and Saturday night housebound: stuck in at home minding baby, drinking lukewarm tea and watching endless repeats of Alan Titchmarsh's *Ground Force*.

There's no need to take such a bleak view of the future. From personal experience I can certainly reassure you, *Ground Force* is not such a bad programme when you get to know the characters. And once you get the Titchmarsh bug it's worth noting he pops up again on Sunday afternoons for *Gardener's World*.

Passenger 58

Most airlines consider flying safe up till the twenty-fifth week of pregnancy, unless the plane crashes, of course. After that time they will require a letter from the doctor to certify that it is unlikely your partner will go into labour at 20,000 feet.

This would be not only less than ideal for the baby but the sight of a barrel-stomached woman stretched across four seats, knickers off and legs akimbo, is enough to put anyone off their complimentary peanuts. Furthermore, a tidal wave of blood and a placental fluid rushing down the aisle could interfere with vital safety procedures such as the queue for a fag in the bog.

This will be a last opportunity to go away for a relaxing break with just the two of you. Find a nice beach in a warm destination and let all the stresses of the last few months wash away. Some mild activity, walks or sightseeing should be fine. Resist the urge to book up any excursions that might involve any strenuous activity for your partner.

The following should be particularly avoided:

1 Mountain trekking/climbing: risk of fall, risk of exhaustion.
2 High diving: risk of world's most spectacular belly flop.
3 Scuba diving: risk of her straying into whale's mating ground and suffering a fate that would've left Jonah begging for excommunication.
4 Skiing: risk of exhaustion, risk of fall, risk of schnapps-sozzled husband slipping on ice and ramming ski-pole up Khyber.
5 Horse riding: risk of loss of virginity.

White Noise

Towards the end of six months, as your partner starts to finally balloon up, it might strike her that this is her last chance to get you into church. Any later and the sight of her waddling down the aisle will become so embarrassingly comic that the risk is that one of the guests will cash in by sending the home video to *You've Been Framed*. Your granny has always been fond of your partner, but let's face it, 250 quid is a lot of anyone's money for thirty seconds of video footage.

If wedding bells are your idea of hell, be aware this is the most testing time. Arcane pressures might be brought to bear to get you down to Hatton Garden with the heavy cheque book.

Prepare arguments for rebuttal such as . . .

'God wouldn't like it. He knows I'm an Arsenal fan.'

'Gay couples don't get married. Why should we?'

'I've got a bad leg.'

'Illegitimacy is not a social stigma, darling. His nursery-school playmates won't sneer and call him a little bastard. Even if they do they're only swearing. They might just as easily call him a little wank-spanner or little bony-assed twat.'

Freshly Laid Plans

As early as the first hospital appointment the consultant will be asking you to decide where you want to have the baby – in hospital or at home.

Statistically there is no medical reason why you can't have the baby at home. But if she wants to have it there, she will probably have to struggle. Doctors don't like making house calls, even to sick people (especially to sick people). It may be they never got over working three-hundred-hour weeks when they were training. Now they're qualified, we can darn well come to them on the bloody stumps of our hands and knees if need be.

If she does decide to plump for a home birth, she will need your help and support to push for it. You can earn Brownie points for suggesting she contacts organisations such as International Home Birth, and the Society to Support Home Confinements. They will help you find a doctor and/or midwife willing to schlep round to your pad for the event. (One such organisation calls itself Association of Radical Midwives, which should be enough to terrify the most intractable health authority.)

The main thing is preparation. It is imperative to decide on a home birth right at the beginning. This is not a situation where once labour starts you can phone the hospital and say, 'So, doc, fancy popping over to ours? We've got plenty of booze left over from the weekend.'

Father-to-be should be happy to take a lead from mum-to-be when discussing location. She might feel more secure in a fully equipped hospital knowing she is a short trolley ride away from the operating theatre. Therefore it's bad form to start protesting: 'I see how that suits you, love, but our due date falls slap bang in the middle of the Cricket World Cup. I've ordered a wide-screen telly and everything . . . Don't be so silly, of course I'll come up and see how you're doing between overs.'

4
Last Three Months: Fat Is a Feminine Issue

Feeling Bubbly

You're starting to think 'any time now'. You don't want to pre-empt anything, but as the last three months of pregnancy hove into view champagne is already on ice. (In fact, this is the second lot of champagne on ice. You drank the first lot when your mate, Alan, came back after the pub one night. The tight-fisted git promised to replace it but never did.)

Everybody seems eager to jump the gun. Relatives telephone daily and ask to be kept informed. The friendly chap from over the road (how much polishing does a 1963 Morris Minor need?) looks up expectantly every time you leave the house as though you're just rushing off to the hospital.

Keep in mind there are a full twelve weeks to go. Just as the league isn't won in January, babies are seldom born in the seventh month. This has less to do with tempting fate than damping down impatience to get the darn thing born. The waiting is going to be bad enough. The waiting is going to be bloody awful. By the finish you'll feel like telling your partner, if you don't hurry up and drop it, I'm sending in a search team.

Don't be swayed by suggestions the baby could be a couple of months premature. Ninety-three per cent of babies are born at full term or later. (The other 7 per cent are born at half-term to keep it quiet from the other pupils.)

Sex With a Space Hopper

One way to pass the long evenings up to the due date is to have plenty of sex.

You've sneaked a look at her undressing for bed and haven't minded at all what you've seen. Her boobs are full and taut. Her skin and hair are glossy and bright. She's more womanly than ever. You're definitely keen, but somehow haven't quite worked out how to tackle the huge Zeppelin strapped to her front. Sadly, this Space Hopper has no ear-handles to help you stay aboard.

There are plenty of ways to make sex comfortable in late pregnancy as long as you're not blinkered towards the missionary position (you know, the one where you put on the Terry Waite mask). Try rear entry, side entry, on all fours, or standing up. The key tenet of 'total football' as practised by the famous Dutch side of the seventies was positional variety. Now is the time to practise 'total sex'.

Almost certainly the most comfortable position is with her on top. Many women find this configuration perfect for some pre-season breast-feeding practice. Her training will comprise manoeuvring her breasts towards your mouth thereby locating the most comfortable angle for having them gently sucked. Your role as breast-feeding coach shouldn't prove unduly onerous. You might even offer an baby-ish sigh of appreciation. But if she wants you to warm her up by donning a nappy and crawling around the bed crying 'goo-goo ga-ga, where's my milk', she can forget the whole thing.

Sex in the last three months may leave your partner feeling unusual sensations down below. But it's unlikely you can celebrate her first orgasm. These are small uterine contractions known as Braxton Hicks or 'rehearsal' contractions. They are brought on because your semen contains prostaglandin hormones. Prostaglandin hormone is what women are given to induce labour when they're overdue. Braxton Hicks contractions cannot bring on full labour unless she's ready to drop anyway.

Pleased as Punch and Judy

Your partner suggests you come along to ante-natal classes run by the hospital. You don't need a second invitation to get the afternoon off work. This all part of the fun.

When you get there you find everyone sitting around in a

circle as though this is some kind of group therapy session. You realise it is a group therapy session and are about to stand up and confess to being an alcoholic when the teacher strolls in.

The teacher is a small, serene woman in pale loose clothing and a preacherly glint in her eye. You scan the faces around the room and discover two things. Firstly, even very ugly people make love to each other and seem pleased at the prospect of replicating themselves. Secondly, everyone else is wearing loose pale clothing and looks impossibly serene. You wonder if you've accidentally joined the Moonies.

Unlike them you are wearing a suit, tie and a thick film of sweat, having rushed over from the office. The woman next to you puts a handkerchief to her nose and you clock on she can smell the alcohol on your breath from that lunch-time pint.

You came here to find out about relaxation but next thing you face is the heart-thumping circuit of introductory speeches. 'Ahem, we're Anthea and Martin, our due date is the fifteenth of August and our baby's going to be a vegan, peace-loving, Buddhist, that shampoos its hair with yak shit.'

Ante-natal classes often consist of half-a-dozen two-hour sessions spread across the last couple of months. Over the weeks you have the opportunity to get to know other couples in the same boat as you. You can swap parenting tips with them or discuss any mutual problems you encounter. After that you'll probably slag them off mercilessly all the way home.

As the course nears its end, you'll notice a couple not turning up and wonder excitedly if they've gone off to have their baby. Then, the next week they turn up still pregnant with some mundane tale about waiting in for the gas man. The following week another couple don't turn up, but it turns out they actually were Moonies and have been beamed up to a spaceship to undergo psychic remodification.

Relaxation techniques are a mainstay of the classes. Dad-to-be will learn too: breathing deeply to cope with pain; stress reduction by individually loosening different muscle groups; meditation to relax. 'No thanks, I won't have a pint tonight. I'm going straight home to put on a caftan and practise my Gregorian chanting . . . Oh, go on, then, just a quick one.'

In one session you'll get to tour the hospital labour ward. This will fascinate as it is the actual place you'll go to have your baby. It's advisable to stick with the group. If you do get lost, knock before entering any wards or you might find yourself roped in to holding the leg of a meaty-thighed Ukrainian woman in the last throes of delivery. 'Help me poosh harder, you cabbage-livered Vestern vimp.'

Forceps, Please

As the tour begins, the serene woman in pale loose clothing encourages you to ask questions. You ask one. 'You know these forceps things, can we see a pair?'

The mask of serenity drops for a moment. 'Later,' comes the abrupt reply.

The tour continues around the ward. Everyone else has questions: they want to see the gas-and-air machine; how the baby's heart monitor works; the vegans want to know if any sheep were hurt in the manufacture of the blankets. Each request is dealt with quickly and politely.

'I'd still like to see a pair of forceps.'

'Sorry. None about.'

You have the impression you are being fobbed off. You can't think why. The phrase 'forceps delivery' was bandied about quite freely in the circle-sitting sessions. So and so had a forceps. If you need a bit of help, they'll use the forceps. You imagine these forceps as like a pair of tweezers; slim silver implements you might slip into a nostril to remove a stray hair.

The tour is beginning to wind up. Any comments or questions?

'What about these forceps. Found a pair yet?' you persist brightly.

Everyone turns to you. Above the silence you hear a low grinding sound and realise it's the serene woman's teeth. The grinding stops and she begins deep breathing.

'Right then, forceps. This *gentleman* wants to see a pair. So let's see if we can find some. Oh yes, here we are.'

Reaching into a cupboard, she pulls out something wrapped in paper. She unwraps the paper and reveals finally the famous forceps. What was the big deal? Exactly like tweezers, except for the fact that they are about four thousand times as big!

Forceps suddenly don't seem like something for removing nose hairs, more something you'd use to hoist the engine from a Bedford van. Forceps are big lumps of ironmongery; two-foot long, clanking machine tools.

Oh, maybe they're not so bad. You could describe them as barbecue tongs. Yes, but only if you lived in the town of Bedrock. You certainly wouldn't fancy having anything that size inserted up your . . .

You look around the room and realise three of the women have fainted, so have two of the men. Another woman has spontaneously gone into labour and, despite insisting for weeks she wants a natural birth, is now demanding an emergency Caesarean.

The rest of the party, along with your own partner, have fled the room. The serene woman fixes you with a cold stare.

'Happy now, sir?'

Fine Tuning Your Birth Plan

Now is the time for you and your partner to nail down your preferences, hammer out a few decisions and a hire a torque wrench to fine tune your birth plan.

Your mental checklist runs something like this:

1 Home or Hospital?
What do you mean home or hospital? I told you to sort this out months ago. If you haven't, it's hospital.

2 Water or Land?
Some hospitals have birthing pools installed in the labour wards, but not many. Even if they do you might need to book it up. The water option is more likely if you've arranged a home birth.

Here is another of those infrequent moments when poor dumb hubby gets to be useful. Your input can range from volunteering to make sure the immersion heater is left on so she can have a nice warm bath during labour, right up to ordering a fancy birthing pool which has the potential for full underwater delivery.

Pools can easily be hired. The idea is you have it delivered a week or two before the due date and keep it until the baby is born. The cost is roughly fifty quid for the first week then just a pound a week from then on.

The pool comes as a kit with a bolt-together metal frame, thermometer, couple of hoses, and a sheet of pond liner. (You get to keep the pond liner as a souvenir, because no one wants to re-use it after you.)

Warm water can be a comfort during contractions and support your partner's weight when she's feeling weak. Bear in mind the pool will take a couple of hours to fill up. The midwife might also suggest you dive in to offer moral support, so keep a pair of trunks handy, unless you particularly want to show off the chap who did the dirty deed.

3 Pain Relief or Natural?

Only relates to your partner, sadly. No pain-relieving drugs are offered to the man. Most delivery wards don't even have a bar.

Some women are pretty worried about the pain of childbirth. They know they are going to want something. Others are confident and say they want a 'natural' i.e. nothing above care and support from the people around them. You might think there's nothing 'natural' about suffering pain. Not many people go to the dentist to have a tooth pulled and refuse any pain relief.

Pain relief is something you are supposed to plan ahead but it seems sensible to keep options open. These are generally three-fold.

Gas and Air (Entonox) – self-service; comes out of a pipe in the wall; doesn't do much; doesn't last long.

Pethidine – nurse injects narcotic in bum; makes partner drowsy and woozy, may make her talk gibberish; lasts two hours.

Epidural – anaesthetist runs in tiny pipe (catheter) next to spinal cord, then pumps in anaesthetic. (Epidural is the place they put it, not the drug, so don't ask if the doc can 'slip you a few epidurals' for your hangover.) A 'good' epidural will completely numb her lower half for four hours and give pain-free childbirth.

There is a minute risk of paralysis if the pipe is shoved in the wrong place, but it is minuscule. Would-be anaesthetists who are horribly cack-handed get weeded out early on in training, along with drug addicts and the partially sighted.

My own wife tried everything. With all of our three kids she had very long difficult labours and ended up having an epidural. In each case it transformed her from a blabbering wreck to someone who could cope fairly comfortably. Also, in each case it took ages to 'locate an anaesthetist' who was 'busy in an emergency operation'. So if you want one, ask as early as possible and then keep insisting till you get it.

4 Standing Up or Lying Down?

She won't be restricted to the birth position you decide, but it pays to be aware of different positions. Try them out at home to reveal any problems.

If your partner wants to squat, she'll need you to hold her under the arms to support her weight. You'll find she's rather heavy. By golly, you damned near put your back out. Suggesting that if she wanted a hod-carrier she should have got herself pregnant by one is asking for trouble. She's bound to agree. If she doesn't, but suddenly blushes, you may have stumbled on some unfortunate truth.

This may not be the most academic tome you've ever read but it does contain one unique theory: the Rodgers Birthing Position Theory. It goes like this: the most comfortable position for birth is directly related to the position in which the child was conceived: i.e. flat on her back conception – flat on her back birth position; her on top during sex – then she squats for birth. More and more popular now is giving birth face down on all fours. It's slightly undignified but apparently very comfortable. The husbands always look rather contented chaps too.

The Rodgers theory also works in reverse. So next time you hear a story about a friend who gave birth in the back seat of the car on the way to the hospital, you'll know why.

5 Birthing Partner

You've been waking early recently: five, five-thirty. You haven't actually got out of bed and done anything useful but you've woken. Usually you never have any trouble sleeping right through the alarm and most of the rush-hour traffic. The Land of Nod is your domain, your patch, your manor. Something must be bothering you.

You reckon you know what it is. You want to bottle out. You are supposed to want to see your baby born, and you do, but . . . But you don't want to see the blood and the tears and the after-birth. You don't want to hear the puffing and panting and crying; the letting-it-all-hang-out. You certainly don't want any strangers to see *you* behaving that way. They may be doctors and mid-wives who've seen it all before, but terribly sorry, on this occa-sion they'll have to miss out. You don't blub or faint in public.

It's okay, though, you have a plan . . . a plan right up there with your usual standards. At the first sign of labour you slip out the front door and scarper towards the nearest bar. If it's 4 a.m. you can head for Smithfield Market – the pubs are open all night round there. When you come back you can claim it must have been the full moon, due any week now, and you just went all loopy like in that film *American Werewolf Drinks Light and Bitter*.

You're thinking of having a coat of arms made up: 'Cometh the hour, runneth the man.'

However, deep in your heart of hearts, you know this is not the way to proceed. If you really don't want to go, grit your teeth and let her know. Now. You might find she doesn't want you there either. She might prefer to have her mum there, or her sis-ter. She might rather have the bloke who runs the whelk stall out-side the Dog and Duck than you.

Actually, forget all that. Just go. You might as well. It really is one of the great experiences of life, up there with Stuart Pearce's penalty celebration against Spain in Euro '96 (you didn't mind blubbing and fainting then).

Baggage To Excess

Another thing they bang on about in ante-natal classes is your partner's hospital bag, which should contain stuff like little blue sponges soaked in Evian to mop her brow during labour and extra nighties and spare pairs of knickers. (From the pictures you've seen of childbirth, she's going to need a bit more than spare knickers.) That's all fine and dandy, but why shouldn't you have a bag of your own? No reason.

Here's a checklist for your bag:

- Cigars – at least one big fat one

- Money for pub

- Mints to mask breath after pub

- Survey of local fast-food restaurants
- Snack of peanuts or chocolate
- Change for coffee machine
- Steel-capped shoes for kicking faulty coffee machine
- Very thick skin
- Big hanky – for nose blowing and brow mopping. There's no way you're going to blub

The serene woman said to have the bag packed no later than thirty-six weeks. That's fine for people who pack for their summer holidays at Easter. A seasoned international traveller like you can leave it till, say . . . ten minutes before you leave? If the baby's born in the porch while you're still hunting around for your *Good Pub Guide* then so be it.

Your partner wants you to bring sandwiches in case the labour is very long, perhaps a flask of soup too. (For yourself. She's not allowed to eat.) You aren't sure. You suspect it is horribly uncool. Unpleasant memories of school trips come flooding back. Everyone else had fifty pence to go down the chip shop, but not your mum, she insisted you take a Tupperware tub of vegetarian lasagne. The shame was awful. You'd rather starve than go through that again.

Try not to get competitive on the bag thing. Just because she has a chunky knapsack ready by the door, it doesn't mean you need a Bravo Two Zero-sized bergen stocked up with a year's supply of tinned food, fold-up camp bed and wide-screen portable telly. Then again, no one could blame you for demanding equality in bag size (dimensions and weight to be ratified by a mutually acceptable third party).

Stretching the Point

A couple of chapters ago you were complaining 'Where's the bump?' Your partner didn't look any different. By the end of pregnancy she's unbelievably huge. She's pumped up so big, Richard Branson wanted to buy advertising space on her. (You were happy to sell some too, but he felt the Virgin logo was somehow incongruous.)

As she waddles hot and exhausted down the street, maternity dress billowing in the breeze, you are sensitive to her sensitivities. You make no mention of tent pegs and guy ropes, or 'roll up, roll up for the greatest show on earth'. Then you blow it. She confesses she wishes she could have a cigarette and you tell her not to be so silly, look what happened to the Hindenburg.

Quips of this nature are not always found amusing. Your partner is having to cope with changes all over her body. Her stomach has developed brown streaks known as stretch marks. A gunpowder line of dark hair has chased up from her pelvis to her navel and might have continued further had her belly button not popped outwards to block its path. Some women fight a losing battle against varicose veins which colonise not just the legs, but can make insertions into the vagina and anus too.

Launch a charm offensive by offering to massage some oil into her stretch marks or remove the shoes from her swollen feet. You could even surprise her by nipping to the chemist and buying a bumper size tub of Preparation H. *'I'd go a million miiiles, just to ease your poor piles . . .'*

One last thing. Recently your partner may have started to suffer from rampant flatulence. You're a bit miffed about this. It's not the smell, or the embarrassing, middle-of-John-Lewis, rip-roaring noise that's bothered you. Just that, well, flatulence was heretofore firmly in your sphere of operation, like abject laziness or having drunken rows at parties in which you contend the NHS is a waste of taxpayers' money, Tony Blair is definitely gay, and the host can shut his fat face otherwise you'll deck him. These are all part of your role as a man.

Likewise, if any farting was needed in this pregnancy you were perfectly capable of handling it. Her almighty guffs have left you feeling passed over, side stepped. She's stealing your thunder. Literally.

Try not to worry. After pregnancy the gunpowder line will disappear, her stretch marks will fade, and with a bit of luck you'll get all the farting duties back to yourself. Come on, mate, no one does it like you do.

The Growing Foetus

Nothing spectacular is happening development wise. The foetus's lungs sort themselves out with something called surfactant, bubbles which stop the lungs collapsing between breaths. This is the same stuff you are busily buggering up by smoking.

What else? Fingernails begin to grow, possibly a mop of hair and that's about it.

What the last three months is really about is growth. The baby will double in length and triple its weight by the time of delivery. Most of this growth occurs in the body to give it a chance to catch up with the head.

Around thirty-six weeks the foetus's head engages in the pelvis, a bit like a spaceship docking, to get ready for exit. Vernix, a kind of axle grease, covers the baby's head and body to protect the skin on the way out. If your partner walks like she's got a big greasy coconut trapped between her thighs that's because she has.

You Can Get the Staff

The foot-and-a-half-long foetus is getting cramped. It doesn't matter how many times you tell it the bijou basement it occupies would go for a hundred grand in Knightsbridge.

The result is precious little room for the other occupants of your partner's body, people like Mr Stomach and the Intestine family. (Bob Bladder has applied for rehousing, but has only been offered the top floor of Janet Street Porter.) The outcome is indigestion and uncomfortable sleeping.

Often you'll turn over in the night and find her awake, bolt upright, lamp on, seventeen pillows at her back, leafing through a library-sized pile of baby books. You'd be worried if you hadn't seen your partner go through so many weird changes and stages over the last months. By now, if Godzilla crept into bed next to you, you'd assume it was merely the spiky-reptile-who-feasts-on-skyscrapers phase of pregnancy.

Take the other night. You woke to find her gone. A strange noise was coming from the kitchen. When you got there you found her halfway up a step-ladder frenetically scrubbing out the kitchen cupboards with a demonic blaze across her eyes. You didn't panic. You didn't shout 'get thee behind me witch', grab some garlic and call 07000 EX-OR-CISE '360 degree head-swivels our speciality'.

You didn't turn a hair, because you knew she was 'nesting'. This is the phenomenon of last-minute frenetic cleaning and home-making in preparation for the hatching of the chick. Instead you slipped back to bed, with thoughts of how to turn her excess energy to your advantage. Tomorrow night you'll leave a bucket and sponge out for her. A helpful note pinned to the front door: 'Don't forget the alloy wheels.'

The Full Nelson

At nine months the baby is ready to be born. On the inside, it's got everything it needs development-wise. On the outside, the baby has a whole new life waiting for it: nursery decorated; cot installed; clothes bought; brand new buggy parked in the drive.

Unfortunately nobody told the baby. It's refusing to come out. Despite warnings to the contrary, you allowed yourself to think the baby would be either early or on time. But no. It's late. Nearly two weeks late. The waiting is driving you bonkers. Winnie Mandela didn't have to wait this long.

You've taken to answering the phone with the words 'No news' because it's always someone inquiring if you've 'become a daddy yet' or 'heard the patter'. People at the office are demanding, 'Bloody hell, surely she's shoved it out by now? Tell her to get a move on.' And if that cheery bloke from over the road looks up expectantly once more, you'll kick fifty-seven varieties of crap out of him, then set fire to his classic car.

5

Labour: Now Is *the Time For All Good Men . . .*

Missouri Breaks

She'll know labour has started because three things happen:

1 A 'show' of bloody mucus appears in her knickers.
2 Her waters break.
3 Contractions start.

You'll know labour has started because:

1 Your mobile phone rings.
2 You almost didn't hear it ring.
3 You've just handed over sixty quid to a tout outside the ground.

'Yeah? . . . What's that? . . . Hang on a minute . . . GO ON MY SON!! . . . AH, YOU'RE CRAP . . . No, not you . . . You've what? . . . You're joking . . . No, no, that's, er, brilliant. . . . Yeah, of course I'm all right to drive . . . I don't suppose you could pick me up . . . No need to rush . . . Oh, you do need to rush. All right, then.'

The next stage is a mad drive to hospital, police sirens wailing in the distance, your partner writhing about on the back seat à la Tim Roth in *Reservoir Dogs*.

Actually, chances are labour will commence under much more mundane circumstances. It will be in the middle of the night when both of you are in bed, sober, and there is plenty of time. This is because one-two-three: show, waters, contractions, normally take many hours to develop. The nearest you get to any drama is the huge row you had because you wanted to go out to a party and she wanted you in bed, sober, with plenty of time.

How To Make an Emergency Delivery

A lot more deliveries take place before the mother makes it to hospital than you might think. There are several hundred in the UK every year. Percentage-wise the odds are still low, but just in case, here's how to make an emergency delivery yourself:

1 Call ambulance 999 (still a free call, although 0898 999 may be just around the corner).
2 Tell partner not to panic (best achieved by running around the room waving hands in the air shouting, 'My God, what are we going to do?').
3 Tell partner to pant to stop her bearing down.
4 Wash your hands and her vagina (in that order).
5 Sit partner against wall, knees up, clean cloth under her bum. (If you're anal enough to start worrying about the new carpet, put bin bags down, don't start hunting around for your policy booklet to see if you're covered for staining.)
6 When head begins to show, tell her to pant, *never pull head*, if anything, slow down head emergence by holding it gently in.
7 If umbilical cord is around neck – slip your finger under it and gently hook it over the baby's head.
8 Tell partner not to push. Instead she should blow like a choo-choo train and hold the baby's head from emerging any more until cord is unhooked.
9 When head is out, gently manoeuvre it backwards (mum's bumwards) till shoulder comes out, then the other way till other shoulder comes out. Once shoulders are out baby will slip out okay.
10 If baby is breathing/moving, lay it on mum's tummy – *keep baby warm* by covering body and head.
   a) If baby is blue/limp, slap its bum or pinch it to make it cry. Crying will make it breathe.
   b) Still not breathing, *very gently* suck on nose/mouth to

clear mucus from airways.
   c) Still not breathing, *very gently* try artificial respiration.
   d) Still not breathing, massage baby's heart by tapping firmly(ish) on ribs twice a second.
11 *Don't pull on cord. Don't cut cord.*
12 Placenta needs to come out. It's attached to the other end of the cord. Once placenta is out, keep it safe in a plastic bag or bowl of water, attached, and slightly above the baby.
13 If partner is bleeding, keep bleeding end lower than her head.

After that you can . . .

14 Wipe brow.
15 Open can of lager.
16 Ask, 'Who's next then?'
17 Keep everyone warm and laughing till the ambulance arrives.

This is all for *emergencies only*. So don't engineer the situation to grab a bit of glory. Anyway, it would take more than one un-assisted act of midwifery to make up for all your bad behaviour over the last few years.

If any of this happens in the car, perform exactly as above with heating on and her on the back seat. And, oh yeah, pull over and switch the engine off first. This is childbirth, not taking a call on your mobile phone.

Announcement Over

Just to welcome back all those people who never bother to listen to the emergency information on planes. The film on this flight is *Karate Kid* 7.

More On How You'll Know

This is how it starts. Imagine the baby is in an upside-down wine box. First thing, the tap of the wine box breaks off and lands in her knickers. That's the show. No need to go to hospital at this stage.

Next she gets contractions, i.e. the opening of the wine box begins to pulsate and widen. (It's a possessed wine box, okay!) No need to go to hospital until the strongest contractions last about thirty seconds.

Next, wine trickles out; the head of the baby is stopping it gushing out. That's the waters breaking. (Or it might just be urine. A sweet, oaky, Chardonnay is the waters breaking. A £4-a-bottle house wine in Bengal Curry Emporium that looks like pee, smells like pee and tastes like pee – *is* pee!) This is the time to call the hospital.

Actually your partner may experience any of the above in any order. Which makes things confusing. The last thing she probably needs is you asking if it's house wine or Lindemans Bin 65.

Labour Isn't Working

Just when you need pregnancy to be straightforward, the whole business gets confusing. Those labour contractions might instead be Braxton Hicks rehearsal contractions. The 'show' may not be noticeable. The waters breaking may just be Bob Bladder complaining about his lack of space again.

Instead of having a distinct identity, labour has a twin brother known as 'false labour'.

In doubt, you sensibly call the hospital. They suggest you come in. Then you spend hours hanging about in some ward till everyone gets bored and turfs you out. As you arrive home the only thing she can feel between her legs is her tail. You both feel ridiculed. All those nurses back there are rolling their eyes and sniggering behind their hands.

Not so.

Let's go back and ask. For a start, the reason the hospital asked you to come in was they didn't know it was false labour either; the same reason they kept you hanging about for hours. Secondly, if it weren't for false labour half the midwives could be sacked. Lastly, the consultant's wife has just given birth on the top table of a rugby club dinner because her husband (three tries and a drop goal) assured her she was in false labour.

New Labour, No Danger

Next day the whole thing starts off again. She can phone the hospital this time. You're not making a prat of yourself again.

The false labour debacle had one silver lining. You don't have to hunt round for your respective pregnancy bags – they are already in the boot of the car.

This time, though, you've caught the rush hour. You wave your fist out the window, swear, and scream that you're in a terrible life or death hurry. The guy at the news stand on the corner recognises you, because you're the bloke who every morning, on his way to work, waves his fist out the window, swears and screams he's in a life or death hurry.

You take an alternative route to the hospital, a few back doubles to cut through the traffic. They don't call you the 'human A to Z' for nothing. A smug grin begins to creep across your mouth when bang! . . . you hit the first of maybe thirty speed bumps down this road.

'Oh my God,' she screams holding her belly. 'I'm going to give birth going over a sleeping policeman.'

'Ah, you'll be all right. If I can just get up to forty miles an hour we'll skip right over them.'

If it wasn't real labour when you started out, it certainly is now.

More Haste, More Speed

Car screeches to a halt, double parked on triple yellow line. Hazards on, horn blaring and (German edition) warning triangle propped up beside boot. You rush into the reception all aflap.

The guy on the reception desk is about to direct you to the labour ward but then says: 'Oh, it's you two. Labour ward's same place as yesterday. Sixth floor.'

The lift not only takes an age to come, but by the time it finally does other people have the temerity to expect they can share it with you. They can think again.

'Hard luck, pal, this an emergency . . . No, I don't care how much blood you're losing . . . You shouldn't have let him shoot you . . . It's not my fault you're only armed with a truncheon.'

Finally you make it to the labour ward. A sleepy-looking nurse looks up from her TV guide.

'Quick, nurse. The baby's coming. Really coming this time.'

'All right, darling, come this way.'

She shows you to a room. She smiles. She turns down the bed. She hunts around for a pillow. She hunts around for a blanket. She hunts for a baby monitor. She connects up the baby monitor. She smiles some more then wanders out to find a doctor to have a look at you. All of this is done with the speed and urgency of a dead ox.

You pay your taxes. Lots of 'em. Where's the speed? Where's the anxiety? You paid for blind panic and you expect blind panic.

Instead, the nurse ambles out of the room and disappears for a long time.

Somewhere deep down you know the nurse isn't panicking because she sees this all the time every day. She knows when to rush and when not to. You are the same in your job. When some new customer comes on the phone demanding goods delivered today, you don't think to yourself, I'll really break my neck for this bloke. You think, sure mate, get in the queue with everyone else.

You decide to use this window of time to move the car from outside the main entrance. (Some blind guy had his guide dog clamped the other day.) You might just have time get it parked properly before the baby is born.

You sprint down, jump in the car, fumbling and dropping keys, rush the car to the car park by carving up a couple of ambulances, deposit about fifty quid in the parking machine before bounding back up six flights of stairs, virtually puking and vowing to sue British American Tobacco for a new set of lungs. Phew!

When you get back to the room seven minutes later, your partner is in exactly the same position. No one's been in. Nothing's happened.

Hands Up Anyone Who Wants To

A few minutes later a nurse comes in, pulls on a pair of medical Marigolds, nods hello and inserts several fingers up your partner's vagina.

Hang on a minute.

You aren't sure where to look. Your wife hardly knows this woman. Is this really necessary? Couldn't she use a medical instrument? Does she need to use her whole hand? Much further and she'll need a pair of waders.

A few minutes later another nurse arrives. She twiddles a few knobs on the baby monitor, adjusts pillows, checks your partner's notes. You glance at a chart on the wall. By the time you glance back, this woman's now copping a feel of your wife's vagina. She's poking around as casually as delving into a pocket for loose change. Maybe she *is* after loose change.

You are about to protest when a doctor shows up. Thank God for that. It's a bloke doctor with a beard and glasses, and a beer belly, but young, no more than, maybe, twenty-eight. He shakes your hand firmly, converses with the delving nurse. Sanity at last.

Then, he's in on the act, jamming a meaty paw up your wife. Crikey Moses, he couldn't wait. The other midwife only just had time to get her hand out.

It's true your partner doesn't seem to mind. And the doctor did warn her first. Sort of. 'I'm going to examine you now.' But he never actually asked permission. He certainly never asked yours. You're not the jealous type, but if some stranger wants to put his hand up your wife, a bit of a 'by-your-leave' might be appreciated. You do have standards.

What's happening here? Well, if you went to the doctor with a boil on your foreskin, he would have to look at it and touch it. You'd expect that. He'd expect it. (Not the highlight of his week maybe, but he'd do it.) What's weird is seeing this transaction occur between two other people. This may be the first time you have been present at someone else's medical examination.

Secondly, you haven't enough information. These 'nurses' are actually midwives. They have done an extra few years medical training to become midwives. They are almost like doctors, but with limitation to 'treat' childbirth.

Thirdly, cervical examinations (via the vagina) are the main way of checking how labour is progressing. The cervix, the entrance to the womb, is contracting and dilating, pulling up and opening so it's big enough for the baby's head. Labour begins when the cervix is 3 cm wide. When it's 10 cm wide, delivery of the baby starts. Midwives and doctors check this by seeing how many fingers they can get in the cervix.

In a long labour there could be several more hands going in there. What with the instruments, probes, and an entire baby coming out, your partner's vagina is going to be busier than the Old Kent Road.

Does He Take Cinnamon?

Labour and birth are different for everyone. Some lucky people whip in, have the baby within an hour and whip out. For many, though, and particularly with first babies, labour is a much longer, more drawn-out process, lasting several hours.

After the initial examination you will be directed to the labour suite, the place you got a tour of a few months back. NHS hospitals use the labour suite to make a good impression. Pea green walls may seem drab to you, as does the 'eclectic' mix of Office World furniture, but compared to the rest of the hospital it's Buckingham Palace.

Home comforts are multitudinous. In other words there's a cubicle down the hall with a kettle and . . . and that's it. The midwife will make great play of the fact that in the cupboard are tea bags (Tesco Value) and instant coffee (do they really still make Mellow Birds?) and, 'Ooh, look, there's even some milk in the fridge.' You nod enthusiastically, thinking, 'How does she expect me to rustle up a double-shot latte with cinnamon shake from that lot?'

Blaming the Sub-Contractor

You spend the next few hours more or less alone to cope for yourselves. Your partner's contractions gradually get stronger and stronger, closer and closer together.

These hours are where you play your big role and, hopefully, win your spurs. For nine months you've been swanking round with the honorary title of 'birthing partner' and now it's time to earn it. This is the bit that you, solely, as husband, partner, father-to-be can fill successfully. Everyone else in the hospital might know more about medical stuff, but only you really know the woman who is about to have your baby.

As labour becomes more intensive for your partner, you need to cuddle and comfort her. You can rub her back and massage her shoulders. You can remind her of all the breathing techniques you were both taught to cope with pain.

(For those suddenly wishing like heck they'd listened more closely, the basic idea is to keep breathing throughout the contractions rather than tense up. You, the birthing partner, repeat rhythmically, 'Keep breathing, keep breathing, go on, keep breathing.' Demonstrate this by breathing yourself. The rhythm and repetitiveness of your voice should be soothing. Don't get carried away and break into an impromptu rap, whereby you begin referring to her as 'my funky-bellied bitch'.)

Between contractions try to take your wife's mind off the next one coming. Chat away, relax her, maybe offer the odd quip. You could try distracting her by reading out a newspaper article. But nothing too complex. The finer points of Faldo's new backswing may bypass her just now.

Also you can offer encouragement. Tell her she's doing well. Give positive instructions. For example, say, 'Good. Excellent. You're doing so well, darling. Well done.' This sounds horribly banal on paper but better than, 'Do you want to end up in agony? Well, do you? 'Cause if you carry on holding your breath like that, agony is exactly what you are going to end up in.'

In a nutshell, you have to be the one that copes emotionally. She doesn't have to. She can scream, cry or swear if she wants. She is at liberty tell you to 'shut up, stop telling your stupid jokes and for God's sake cut the crap with all this "you're doing well, darling" stuff.' You might feel she hates you. She doesn't. All right, she does. But she needs someone to hate right now, so let her.

Giving support means checking back your own feelings so you can respond to hers. Not an easy job. You thought your role as a bloke was to be amusingly selfish, boorish and intractable. It's served you well enough up to now. Surely others will handle all that support-giving malarkey.

Surprisingly, when the time comes you should find this role both easy and rewarding. In concerning yourself with her feelings you have less time to worry about your own. Quite nice to play second fiddle once in while. Just for a few hours. When it's all over, you can always go back to being a selfish sod again.

Half A Minute, Please

Somewhere along the line your partner might have a bad thirty seconds. She may turn to you in cold terror and say with absolute seriousness, 'I can't do this, I can't cope. Please, please, save me from this.'

A scary moment. What on earth do you say? 'Come on then, get your coat, we're going home.' No good. Backing out is not an option.

If this occurs, it will likely do so quite early in labour. Rather than an actual inability to cope at that moment, it's half a minute of blind fear of what is to come. Nine months of mental preparation have come to a head. Once she's into it, she'll find a way to cope.

You could remind her of pain relief available, and of medical care and support. Probable best advice is to mumble something like 'Ah, you'll be all right, love' and wait for the bad thirty seconds to tick away.

Too Good To Go Down

If the labour is deemed poorly established after initial examinations you'll be admitted to a 'preliminary ward'. This is a halfway house for people who are too far gone be sent home (as in false labour) but not far enough to be allowed to clog up the labour suite.

The preliminary ward is just a normal ward but with pregnancy cases rather than sick people, i.e. people waiting to go into full labour and long-term residents, women who are at high risk of miscarriage. It's not the foyer of the Hilton but at least it's not the bedlam of casualty. You won't have to share it with the usual black-eyed drunks and children with javelins through their heads.

A preliminary ward stint is a bit of a come down. You want to get along to the delivery ward proper. You came in full of excitement and this feels like nasty demotion.

But even here your partner will be getting quite strong contractions. You need to be on your game with the comforting and cuddling, even though for the ward's long-term residents life is going on as normal. It can be off-putting to embark on one of life's most poignant times, while across the ward two women are fighting over the last fig roll from the tea trolley.

Midwives' Choice

Intermittently a midwife will visit to assess how labour is progressing. She times the length of the contractions, also the gap between them. She answers questions and offers plenty of encouragement to you both.

As the long hours go on, you become quite attached to her. You start to call her 'Miranda', the name on her badge. You like Miranda. Miranda becomes very important to you. You discuss calling the baby 'Miranda', if it's a girl. Then suddenly another midwife comes in the room and announces herself as 'Kate'.

'Where's Miranda?'

'Miranda? She went off shift half an hour ago.'

'Oh. Right.'

You eye this Kate with some distaste. She's bright and breezy enough, but she's not as kindly looking. She seems a bit clumsier too, a bit brusque with the pillow plumping. She'll never be Miranda.

One minute Miranda was the most important person in your lives, your treasured supporter, your mentor, and, yes, your rock. The next minute she's slung her hook off to some all-night nurses' pub to snog muscle-bound builders and get slaughtered on triple Southern Comforts. Bloody brilliant.

The good news is that within a couple of hours, Kate will have taken on all the miraculous qualities of Miranda. (Miranda? Huh! You wouldn't saddle a diseased goldfish with a such a stupid name.) It was just that in this intense and emotional time you are very 'open' to other people, particularly people who can offer a clue to what's going on.

However dedicated the medical staff are, they have lives outside and have to finish work some time. For a few hours Miranda held your life in her two hands – now one hand is cupping a Marlboro Light and the other is halfway down the trousers of Mickey the Brickie from Basildon.

Mission Control

You know you've really arrived as birthers when you make it at last into a delivery room. Your partner gets to climb on to the 'bridge', the fancy adjustable bed: reclining head end, collapsing foot end, slots for stirrups. Probes are strapped to her tummy and linked up to a machine by the bed. There's a gas-and-air machine, a resuscitation unit, a blood-pressure gauge. You just wish your car had this many extras.

The tummy probes are the highlight. One gadget lets you follow the fluctuations of the baby's heartbeat. Another shows the peaks and troughs of the uterine contractions – actually prints out a wiggly line on a long stream of graph paper, just like in the movies. Scrutinising this information allows you to follow the contractions as minutely as she does. Often you can see one coming before your partner does, then follow it up to its peak before the line scratches its way back down to zero.

It's easy to become entranced by the vicarious thrill of this – rather than concentrating on supporting your partner.

'Yes, darling, one's coming. The last one was big, but see if you can top it. You've shown me K2 but now I want Everest. Break that record for me, babe.'

All the fun with none of the pain. What could be better?

Heartbeat, Why Do You Miss?

On the same piece of graph paper is a second wiggly line monitoring the baby's heartbeat. This should stay fairly constant at around 130–150 beats per minute. The heartbeat of a foetus in distress will rise and fall more sharply, down to say 60 bpm.

The foetal heart graph may suddenly drop down to nothing. All this normally means is the tummy probe has slipped out of position, i.e. the baby's heartbeat is still there but is not being recorded.

This happened to my wife and me with our first child. We were obviously worried but did not rush out to find the midwife. Finally when she returned, I plucked up courage and said, after clearing my throat, 'Excuse me but our baby doesn't seem to have a heartbeat.'

The midwife merely nodded and moved the probe around until the heartbeat picked up again. Our heartbeats started again too.

The point is that we were pathetically unassertive. We were terrified but said nothing. I fancied myself a fairly forthright guy. I could argue all night over an extra portion of mangetout on a restaurant bill but, when it came to the life of our unborn baby, I had all the courage of . . . of a portion of mangetout.

Must be something about fear of institutions, or people in uniforms, or being a man in a woman's domain. It's a mixture of Freud, Jung and . . . Sod all that psychobabble. Part of your job is to be the assertive one, the complainer. Keep calm, keep polite, and if an argument is brewing do it outside the delivery room so as not to upset your partner. But if you want to know something, damn well ask! And when you're done, demand a complimentary round of Remy Martins for your trouble.

6

Delivery: Blood, Guts and Tin Helmets

Parcel Force

If labour was a curious triple bill of *Beaches*, *Bambi* and *Bridge Over the River Kwai*, then delivery is the last act of *Rocky*. It's rough and physical, with plenty of blood flying about and a final moment of unbounded glory.

The emotional strife of labour is a long and tiring affair. Delivery is quick and exciting. The stage between the cervix having fully dilated (10 cm) to a completed birth may last an hour but feels much less.

Suddenly the delivery room has become very crowded. Everyone pitches in to get the piano down the stairs. Your partner will be pushing for all her might, you'll be gripping one of her legs to give her something to push against, a midwife will be holding another leg, another midwife and possibly a doctor will be at the coal face manoeuvring the baby's head.

You wonder where all these people came from. They made themselves scarce during the long boring bit, but once the main event began they all charged in to claim ringside seats.

Viewpoint

You are really into the experience now. As you grapple with your partner's shank, you genuinely feel part of the medical team.

But you also feel rather hard done by because no one's offered you a mask and gown. They all get to wear the clobber – why shouldn't you? And what about the looks they gave you when you asked where you could scrub up? They claimed there was no need, but you reckon the sinister truth was they'd probably run out of Swarfega.

At one point you inadvertently call out, 'Swab, nurse,' for your perspiring brow.

'I'm afraid you have to be a doctor for the swab treatment.'

'Oh please, just a quick dab. I promise I won't have you struck off.'

'Sorry, the general public have to make do with their sleeves.'

So it appears that holding a leg does not have the kudos of brain surgery. But at least it secures you your own ringside seat. You're close enough to shout encouragement, urging your partner to 'give one more big push'.

You are so busy marvelling at the birth you might feel guilty about neglecting you partner emotionally. Don't worry, she is likely to be too far gone to even know who you are by this point. Instead, keep a firm eye on the exit door. Your baby will only come out once, with no curtain calls.

Keep in mind you have an important role as witness to these events. Her mental state and physical position afford her a far inferior vantage point than yours. She may be doing it but you have the best view of it. If you want an account of the Bruno v Tyson fight, you ask Harry Carpenter. All Frank saw was this big glove, then everything went dark.

Of course, you may not fancy being down the wet end and are content to partake in some dainty encouragement work at the head end. Brow-mopping, face-fanning, and platitude-whispering are all ways to pass the time, particularly if you are starting to come over queasy. Enough bodily fluids are sloshing around without you emptying last night's Pepperoni Feast into the proceedings.

But, really, there's nothing too shocking going to happen down the business end. Having said that . . .

Unscheduled Delivery

Your partner is doing her best to push the baby out of her womb. This pushing is exactly the same as when you've got constipation. Your partner may well suffer constipation late in pregnancy.

70

Think about it . . .

With a bit of luck you've added one and one and come up with two. Number two, actually, because during delivery she will probably do a pooh. She can't help it. It's no big deal. The midwife will clear it up. Or you can . . . Okay, the midwife will clear it up.

Your partner, despite everything, may feel embarrassed by this. You and the midwife will obviously reassure her that nobody minds. It's fair to say you didn't greet the arrival of the turd with the same boundless joy as you will the baby but, really, relax. It happens.

Never let your partner suspect this is something you'll be discussing in the pub with your mates afterwards: 'The baby may have been small but the bowel movement my wife produced more than made up for it. It was like a teddy bear's leg.'

Her embarrassment is probably worse because nobody said anything beforehand. The serene woman who took the antenatal classes was excellent on relaxation and Evian-soaked sponges. Curling one on to the bedclothes during delivery was something she neglected to mention.

But now you know.

Coming Unstuck

If the baby gets stuck, either because the cervix refuses to fully dilate or the head is too big, this is where the famous forceps come into operation. They may look medieval to you, but only in the way that the rack looks medieval, or thumbscrews. Actually they were invented very recently, as long as you call 1600 very recently.

An alternative to forceps is the ventouse extraction (state of the art 1950s' technology), where a metal cap is put on the baby's head, the air is pumped out of the cap via a rubber hose to make a vacuum, then the midwives pull like hell on the hose to get the baby out.

If all this sounds low-tech, it is. But no one's figured out a better way of doing it, which is surprising when as many as twenty per cent of deliveries need assistance. The baby will probably have some welts on its head from the implements but they fade after a few days.

The ultimate stuck baby is one that has to be removed by Caesarean section. They slit open your partner's belly, reach right in there and get the baby out. In extreme emergency these are done under general anaesthetic. Otherwise she may remain awake with an epidural, which also means you can be in the operating theatre to see your baby born.

Twenty years ago Caesareans accounted for five per cent of deliveries. Now it's more like fifteen per cent and rising. (In America it's thirty per cent and rising.) Maybe this is because better nutrition means bigger babies. Maybe today's women are less keen on the idea of struggling to expel a seven-and-a-half-pound human personage. As long as they let us put the sperm in the old way, maybe we shouldn't worry.

A Caesarean section does have a slightly higher risk than normal vaginal delivery. But the procedure is now relatively routine.

Caesarean is so named after Julius Caesar, who was born this way. His mother, Marcia, was obviously 'too posh to push'. Caesar himself, once lifted out of her abdomen, apparently exclaimed:

'Hurry up and get that cord cut, doc, I've got an orgy to go to. The invite said, "Bring a bottle and a still-throbbing placenta." '

Climax

The climax begins when the top of the baby's head appears at the mouth of the vagina. The medical term for this is 'crowning'. (In a 'breach', or upside-down birth, the first thing to show is the buttocks. The medical term for this should be 'mooning' but it isn't. It's still called crowning.)

Once the baby crowns, the midwife will slow the emergence of the head to reduce damage (tearing) to the vagina. If the baby gets stuck at this point she may perform an episiotomy, i.e. cut the skin to allow the head to come out more easily.

After a few pushes the baby's head comes out, followed shortly by the body. And there you are. You are a dad. In that moment you may feel a surge of love. You may be shocked to discover your baby looks remarkably like you, a miniature scrunchy-faced version of yours truly.

Physical responses from the father vary:

crying with joy	32 per cent
fainting with joy	28 per cent
punching the air with joy	22 per cent
farting with joy	14 per cent
demanding to know who the real father is	4 per cent

MY GOD — IT REALLY IS A BUN IN THE OVEN!

Aftermath

When the baby emerges it will need a clean up. The midwife may need to pop it in the resuscitation machine to vacuum out mucus from the baby's nose and mouth. She will also wipe the baby's skin which is usually streaked with placental blood and sticky white vernix. This is all part of the midwife's service so there is no need to offer a tip.

The baby will still be attached by the umbilical cord to the placenta. The good news is the baby works just as well in 'cordless' mode – it just has to be cut. Ask if you can cut the cord yourself (I never asked and was only offered on the third and last time). The cord is surprisingly tough and gristly. It's one of those things you have to try at least once, like swallowing the tequila worm and having sex with a goat.

Vegetarian Curry

Your partner still has to push the placenta out. Often an injection is given to her to make the womb contract rapidly and get the afterbirth out quicker.

Placenta contains lots of nutrients and hormones. For this

reason many mammals eat it straight after the birth. You can too. It looks like a pound of raw liver (and actually tastes like it), which may suggest frying it with bacon and onions but it is best cooked as a curry:

Recipe:
1 placenta - approx. 500g
Butter ghee 100g
Spinach - large tin (preferably dented)
Onion - medium
Curry powder - plenty
Anything else you can think of
Serves four (for parties, you can eke out placenta with mince. Not that anyone will turn up)

Chop and fry placenta till brown, add the other stuff, hold nose and eat. Within five minutes you will not only feel wonderfully invigorated but will also be violently sick and turn vegetarian.

Watch the Birdie

An important role for the father is to be the recorder of the event. Make sure you have a camera and plenty of film (i.e. more than three shots) in your pregnancy bag. The level of intrusiveness is a matter for you and your partner. You might want a shot of her doubled up with labour pains but expect to have the camera snatched out of your hand and rammed somewhere painful.

On delivery you have to decide on taste grounds whether to settle for a discrete angle of knees and bedclothes, whereby a compact camera with inbuilt flash gun will suffice, or to swoop in towards the business end for some gory gynaecological close ups. These are best captured with a fast film, wide angle lens and a set of fisherman's oil-skins.

The trendier among you might want to go for a more unusual rendition of the event. Why not take some charcoal and attempt a Gerald Scarfe sketch? A modernist Jackson Pollock interpretation can be achieved quite easily. Wedge a fresh canvas between your partner's knees and wait for it to paint itself. Not sick enough for the Royal Academy perhaps, but the Turner Prize beckons.

The latest thing is to video the birth, so little junior can get a first-hand view of the gooseberry bush he was found under. Problem: how do you video what's going on while simultaneously holding one of your partner's legs and cutting the cord? A fixed camera on a tripod might do it, but it's not very flexible in a crowded room.

Solution: use that Greek bloke who did your cousin's wedding. He was a bit fat and sweaty (not that it stopped your sister getting off with him) but he did a fantastic job.

'Okay, big smile, everyone. Mum, Dad, and you with the beard . . . yes, you, Rolf Harris, give me a big smile . . . Now that's what I call a big smile.'

It could work. And what if you hired David Attenborough to do a voice-over commentary? That would give it some class.

'Here it is in its natural habitat. Is it friendly, we ask ourselves? Or does it bite? Let's go in for a closer look.'

Bonding

The first few hours with your baby are a special time. You are coming to terms with the realisation that you are parents. She is a mother and you are a father. You try it on for size.

'Quickly, Father, wake up! The stables are on fire.'
'Rouse the men and meet me there in five minutes.'

Or maybe:
'Pops, sorry to wake you. Can I take the car to the beach?'
'Sure, son, take the convertible.'

Or possibly:
'Papa!'
'Nicole?'

Or more likely:
'Get out of bed, Dad, before I shoot you out.'
'I swear, son, I've never seen this woman in my life before.'

But those first hours are a special time. The thrill of the birth lingers in the memory. You are in awe of the newborn child. Tiny hands and feet, delicate arms and legs.

The baby is understandably overwhelmed by its new universe. Like you it is certain only of one thing: it badly needs a drink . . . 'Preferably something on draft. Otherwise get me a bottle. Yeah, anything. No, I don't need a glass.'

Come on, this really is a special time. The three of you can integrate your profound feelings of . . . and, erm, intense sensations of . . . oh, you know. Bonding is the technical term. There's no need to be embarrassed about it. (For God's sake, you've had enough practice recently.)

Your name's Bond. Let's Bond. You're licensed to empathise. You're going to need that licence too, 007. The in-laws are coming.

7

The Hospital Stay: In-laws and Out-patients

Victorian Dad

For a while after the birth they allow you to collect yourselves in the delivery room. Just the three of you, dad, mum and tiny baby, sitting quietly in a dimly lit room trying to make sense of what's just occurred. All three of you feel like you've been dragged through a hedge backwards, and one of you actually has.

A few minutes later, a midwife peeps her head around the door. Nice to know you are in caring hands.

'Come along now, everybody out! We need this room for the next lot. Haven't you all got homes to go to?'

Any further rest and recuperation will have to be conducted in the less salubrious surroundings of a maternity ward. Some city centre hospitals survive from Victorian times, fully preserved with fifty-bed dormitory wards, dingy lighting and rattling pipes. Every now and again a man in a tall black hat comes around.

'Get your leeches, lovely leeches. Fat and juicy, farthing a dozen. Slip down a treat with a nice drop of chloroform.'

Whatever the decor, mum will be relieved to get in a nice comfy hospital bed. Beside her, new baby is allocated a cot (in hospital this is a plastic fish tank perched on top of a tea trolley). Your own recovery must be achieved on a three-legged plastic chair, wedged between the bed and a 3,000-watt storage heater.

Shortly afterwards the midwife comes along with a couple of items she thinks might be yours. They seem vaguely familiar. Oh yes, your labour bags. You'd forgotten all about them.

You glance in at the untouched contents of her bag. Hmm . . . Somehow amongst all the blood, sweat and tears, the Travel Scrabble must have slipped your minds. Shame because 'vagina' uses all seven letters, and 'cervix' on a triple word score would surely have sealed the game. But what's this, the natural sponge soaked in mineral water? How could you forget? A couple of dabs with that and she'd never have needed that epidural.

Your own bag proved just as useless. You do a mental checklist. Cigar, still unsmoked. Not allowed. What do hospitals actually have against smoking anyway? Money for pub, mints for breath, survey of local fast-food restaurants. If only you'd had the bottle to use them.

'Nurse, would you mind keeping an eye on my wife for a while? I'm just nipping off for a bite and a couple of pints . . . By the way, give us a light, will you?'

You did eat the chocolate and the peanuts, though. Unfortunately you ate them last week stuck in a traffic jam on the M25. Come to think of it, you're starving. Never again will you let your partner talk you out of making sandwiches. And you'd kill for a flask of soup.

It's Your Call

Gradually the outside world filters back into your consciousness. You've been so wrapped up in events you've almost forgotten that dozens of relatives are anxiously waiting for news.

You hand your mobile phone to your partner, when some bloke from the next bed explains it won't work in hospital. Apparently it screws up the hospital's monitoring equipment.

Great. Hospital is a place where you are away from home, bedridden, and in need of regularly relaying important news to the outside world, but your mobile phone signal is blocked. Don't they realise this is the age of independent communication, the information super highway? With a mobile phone you can order a pizza from the top of Mount Everest (. . . your advert does say 'free delivery') or put on a bet from the middle of a Scottish loch (. . . so that's a tenner for me at 50,000 to one, and a fiver for my mate Nessie) but you can't tell your parents you've become a father from the local General.

Who Should Be the First To Know? Part II

Following the tradition of 'Who should be the first to know? Part I' (news of the pregnancy), it should again be the biker from the upstairs flat. Unfortunately he's currently uncontactable having been remanded in custody for GBH. It will have to be her mum. Or her sister. Or your mum.

'Hello, Mum . . . Yeah, fine . . . Just phoning to . . . What? I would never tell Auntie Ada to "sod off, you nosy old boot and wait for news like everyone else" . . . Not in a million years would those words pass my lips . . . Not loudly, anyway. I even put my hand over the mouthpiece.'

In the Zone

In the post-delivery period a warm glow surrounds everyone. The ward may be hot and cramped and you may be both hungry and tired, but for the rest of that day nothing, but nothing, can bother you.

Then her mum and dad turn up.

But not even they can wind you up. You watch them greet their daughter and their new grandchild with love and affection. Even you get a kiss and handshake. They are genuinely proud of you both. As the four of you gaze lovingly at the little bundle in the fish tank, you feel nothing can spoil it.

Then your mum and dad turn up.

Immediately you see the flash across your mother's eyes when she realises she has been beaten to the punch by her opposite number. Your dad sees that flash too. In that moment you know Satan walks the earth. One of two things are about to occur: either your mum turns on her heel and walks out or she will draw a hatchet from her thigh and send it spinning towards your mother-in-law's temple.

But none of it. She quickly breaks into a smile. Your partner's mother returns the smile and beckons her to the cot. Everyone gets on like a house on fire. Your mum does mention the Auntie Ada incident again, but you promise to apologise and personally invite her to visit.

Everyone is chatting happily. The grandads are talking horse racing and property. All right, her dad is talking property and your dad is remarking he could have bought a house with all the money he's done down the bookies. But it's good to talk. Any minute her mum might turn to your dad: 'You're such a nice chap really. We should never have accused you of burgling our house. It was just that your wife's diamond and ruby necklace looked so familiar.'

'No need to apologise. But, hey, why do I need to steal diamond and ruby necklaces when I can buy them down the pub for twenty quid?'

'That's all settled then.'

The perfect zone is all powerful. Life is like this. Sometimes. Enjoy it while it lasts.

Alone Again

Everyone needs sleep. Your wife will need some and so will you. She can stay overnight in hospital with your new baby. But, as the night time arrives, you must kiss them gently and say goodbye. It's time to go home alone.

It's a poignant moment as you drive home from the hospital through quiet desolate streets. You finally have a chance to think of only yourself. You have become a father. A proper responsible grown up. A family man.

You hardly notice the journey as images of the birth flutter across your mind. Traffic lights may say green for go, but you remain stationary and red-eyed as the emotions of the day well up.

Then some bloke in a Cavalier overtakes, blaring his horn and giving you the finger. You realise with a silent chuckle that the outside world goes on as ever, as ever, as ever. Let it. You can't be disturbed. Not this night. Bloke was probably pissed anyway. Wanker.

Visiting Hours (and Hours)

By next day, word has spread. The extended family start to show up. They come in their droves. There's uncles and aunts and great uncles and great great aunts. Lots of cousins come too, many of whom bring their kids and, while there, meet second and third cousins they haven't seen for ages and ages. Both sets of grandparents come again, of course, every day at least twice.

Your partner's friends come, as do her old schoolfriends and friends from work. Local friends, friends from the north, even friends from Australia who happen to be over. At one point some woman you've never heard of arrives. She turns out to be someone your partner met in a coffee bar in Brent Cross. How many more people can possibly arrive? The only thing that surprises you is that nosy woman from the launderette hasn't turned up. And then, of course, she does come, bringing not flowers but a bag of clothes from a service wash you left there six months ago. You give her the £2.50.

The only set of people who can be relied on not to turn up at all are any of your mates.

'So, Alan, you coming over for a visit?'

'Not this week, I'm snowed under, like. I'm talking about completely Eskimo snowed under; burst pipes in my igloo; anti-freeze leaking out of my huskies . . .'

'But you're unemployed.'

'So true! How do people find time to go to work? Okay, I'll try and get up to the hospital . . . But if I don't, I'll definitely see you down the pub, eh?'

'Please come. All her mates have come.'

'Okay. I'll come. You can rely on me . . . Actually you can't. I hate hospitals. Place you go to die, ain't it.'

'But, mate, you're only twenty-seven.'

'Hospitals don't respect your youth. You might skip in full of the joys of spring, but on the way out you're horizontal between brass handles and a bloke in a black crombie is whistling the theme tune to *Titanic*.'

'All right. But you are pleased for me, aren't you?'

''Course I am, mate. Brilliant news. Fantastic . . . By the way, have you had a chance to speak to the bloke who does them cheap car-seat covers yet?'

At least the launderette woman was original. Everyone else brings flowers. Thousands of them, bunches, bouquets, sprays, plants. I mean, what use is that lot? You've sniffed one flower you've sniffed 'em all. A couple of people brought helium balloons and three brought chocolates. But where are the cases of the wine and champagne? Where are the Petit Fours and cartons of fags? Two hundred Bensons with 'It's a Boy' plastered across the side would go down a treat.

You're not that bothered really. You don't mind visitors. It's nice they all care enough to come. But why, oh why, do they have to stay for so damn long? Each visitor seems to think they have to stay for a minimum of an hour.

Sometimes a lot longer. Nearly everyone stays until the next lot of visitors have arrived, like it's some marathon relay for the *Guinness Book of Records*. They all expect to be entertained as well. If you have to talk another aunt through the delivery again you'll go mad.

'Do you mind whipping up the bedclothes, darling, Aunt Mabel wants to inspect your stitches . . .'

'Oh, that's lovely needlework. Knit one, pearl two, then a double seam around the anus.'

And the next old duffer that asks, 'Where can you get a decent cuppa round here?' – expecting you to dart off to the canteen – will genuinely find themselves leaving horizontal between brass handles.

Sign of the Times

How do you broach this subject without upsetting anyone? How do you make it clear that actually your partner is just a teensy bit tired after the birth? Particularly as the baby is keeping her awake at night. Not to mention the other four thousand babies on the ward.

There are ways. You could put a sign above the bed. Hospital Visiting Times: Ten Minutes – Then Bugger Off. Alternatively, you could get the hospital to switch all the lights out, bolt the door and pretend you are all out.

The sensible approach is tell them straight out. You are rather fatigued, you've had a lot of visitors and could they kindly not stay too long. If you explain slowly and carefully enough no one will be offended.

Then again, the 'bugger off' sign above the bed is much simpler. Particularly if enforced with steel-tipped winkle-picker up the jacksie.

Relief At Hand

Going home in the evenings, the empty house may feel a bit quiet. You get to escape the relatives at least, unlike your partner. You take the opportunity to really relax. Crack open a bottle of something nice, kick your shoes off and slump down into the warm enveloping grasp of your sofa. You pat the familiar cloth affectionately.

'I've missed you, my old sofa,' you say aloud. Then quickly you glance at the window, hoping no one's looking in. There is someone looking in. It's another relative. It's her brother come down from university.

'Watch'a, dad,' he bellows when you open the front door. 'Got your carpet slippers on? Need a light for your pipe? Give us a hand with my bags and I've got a nice bag of Werthers Originals for you.'

His bags? His bags! Turns out your partner said he could stay with you while he was down. You groan inwardly. Not only is your peace shattered but her brother is hardly the perfect house guest. He's noisy, he's greedy, he smells and . . . and you're sure there was something else. At least he hasn't brought his horrible dog with him. Last time, that damned dog did a crap under your bonsai tree.

'Dog's not well,' he explains.

'Oh dear, that's a shame.'

'Yeah, so can you give us a hand to carry him out of the taxi? And you wouldn't have a fiver for the driver, would you?'

That was the other thing: he's tight.

End of the Tunnel

During the hospital stay, when not fending off visitors, or catering for house guests, you are farming telephone calls from more people who want a blow-by-blow account of the birth. The relatives and well-wishers will continue to pester you for many weeks even after you've brought your baby home. At least there you can pretend to be out.

There is one way to markedly reduce this flow in the post-delivery period. That is to have another baby next year. Somehow the second baby never garners quite the same interest. Visitors are less, flowers are less, interest is less. Remembering the response to your first baby you can actually hark fondly back to the influx of kinsmen and clan. (The house guest scenario is often worse. An extended stay by one of the in-laws to 'help with your other children' may or may not be a welcome assistance.)

If news of a third pregnancy ever spills from your lips, the best response you can hope for is, 'What's wrong with you two? Haven't you got a telly?'

Baby Gazing

In amongst this mayhem is your new baby. He or she is ostensibly the centre of attention but you sometimes wonder if they are just the excuse for the latest round of family get-togethers. Births, marriages and deaths are milestones for the active participants;

for everyone else they are an excuse for a chin-wag and a few drinks.

Obviously you spend a lot of time just gazing at your baby in wonder. Newborn babies don't do much. They don't perform a lot in the way of party tricks. But they remain endlessly fascinating, merely by being alive.

Every little blink of the eye or twitch of the mouth is testament to its reality. The tiny chest breathes up and down. The miniature hands with their tincy fingers and microscopic fingernails grip around your fat stubby thumb like it was an entire arm. This human being works. It's alive. And it's yours for ever. Amazing to think all this started from three minutes of bonking nine months ago. It probably wasn't even very tender bonking. Surely it can't have been the time she told you off for humming the theme tune to *Baywatch*?

Breaking the Mould

For the first few days in hospital, you will spend much time holding your new baby. Which is nice, but not very easy because the baby is so flaccid and apparently fragile. You are frightened to hold the baby too tight in case you crush it but if you hold it too loose the head flops down alarmingly. Someone will one day invent a holder for newborn babies, or a mould. Till then the method is to hold the body with one hand and support the head with the other, or alternatively to lean back in a chair while resting the entire baby on your chest.

Fortunately, midwives are used to new parents and realise you know absolutely nothing. They are happy to show you how to change your baby's nappy, dress it and bathe it. (To put it another way, they reckon you better learn to care for your baby as soon as possible, because they haven't got time to do it.)

Nappy changing a newborn takes a few minutes and some care (details in next chapter). Within a few weeks you will be changing a nappy in a few seconds and could do it blindfold.

Human Yo-Yo

Staying in an NHS hospital is not much fun unless you are lucky enough to get a private room. Your partner is sleeping (or not) in a dormitory with a lot of other mums and a lot of other babies.

She may appreciate some decent food brought in. Even a take-

Ke^rer

WHo's GoT HiS DADDY'S EYES THEN?

away. McDonald's will feel like Michelin three stars compared to the slop they serve up in hospital. You know: lumpy mashed potato served with an ice-cream scoop, soggy cabbage and steak and afterbirth pie. Actually, it's not bad considering it was prepared in a building forty miles away, by a company called Borstal Catering.

Borstal Catering as a private company is committed to customer care. When you leave hospital you will get a form asking for comments.

Did you find the food:

1 good
2 okay
3 poor
4 regurgitate and enclose in pre-paid envelope provided
(We call this customer feedback.)

Little surprises, like bringing your partner in a take-away, can easily be forgotten with all the other things you are required to ferry up and down from the hospital. She will need night-clothes for her, night-clothes for the baby, various creams, lotions, books. The list is endless. You don't know where any of the stuff is in the house, so you end up bringing what you can find, which is always wrong. It's not easy being a dad these first few days. You'll be pretty busy when you've brought them home too. So make sure you arrange something nice for yourself.

Wetting the Baby's Head

It's a known fact that newborn babies suffer from a dry scalp called 'cradle cap'. The only cure is to apply a special moisturiser called lager directly to the tongue of the newborn's father.

The tradition of 'wetting the baby's head' comes from baptism. In times gone by, when infant mortality rates were very high, it was normal to have a baby baptised as soon as it was born. This sacrament of purification cleansed the child from original sin and allowed it in the event of death to enter the kingdom of God. These days we have adapted the ceremony to be a last touching opportunity to get absolutely shit-faced with your mates before the burden of fatherhood weighs in.

Any Baptists out there will know it's not enough just to have a few drinks. They must go for total immersion in a vat full, following the tradition of St Oliver of Reed, who met Jesus wading across the river Euphrates and asked him if he could do that water-into-wine trick again.

A few simple rules to make sure head-wetting goes well:

Dos
1 Number one most important rule: do it soon. Do it while your partner and baby are still in hospital. If you leave it till they come out you'll always be worrying about staying out too late, getting too drunk, staggering into the nursery and puking into the baby's cot. If you put it off, you'll either never get round to it or leave it so long that the baby will be old enough not just to come with you but to stand its own round.
2 Detail one of your mates to arrange it. You'll be too busy running up and down the hospital. (Your mobile doesn't work there, remember.) Make a pact with the mate to do the arranging for you well before the delivery date. All you should need to worry about is turning up at the pub at whatever time you can make it and know that other people will be there.
3 Do make specific plans. Get your mate who's doing the arranging to set day, time and place. Impress on people it's important they turn up. Head-wetting is a vital part of British

culture, right up there with eating vindaloo, drinking Kronenberg and smoking Marlboro.

4 Do have a few beers and enjoy yourself.

Don'ts

1 Don't get confused with the idea that this is a stag night. You don't need to be so drunk you end up chained to a lamp-post with a bog seat round your neck. Impress on your mate that's doing the arranging, there's no need to order a stripper. After what you've been through you won't feel like sexually objectifying a woman's body. Your mates will still cry out 'Ooh', 'Aah' and 'Who nicked the blade out your strimmer?' You, however, can merely remark, 'You see the labia majoris, well, the cervix is situated about six centimetres above that and the uterus lies – 'Shut it, mate!'

2 Don't get so drunk you end up getting off with the barmaid. This is seriously bad form and is liable to result in an appearance on the *Jerry Springer Show* with the caption, 'As she gave birth, he played away' . . . or possibly 'Mum was laid up – Dad got laid' . . . or even 'I breastfed our baby – he feasted on some slapper's tits.'

3 Don't get so carried away with your description of the delivery that you begin passing around the gory pictures of your wife giving birth. 'You see the labia majoris, well, the cervix is situated . . .'

4 Don't mention the pooh.

8

Coming Home:
Oh My God, It's Alive

Awkward Squad

Childbirth is obviously, inescapably gynaecological. Equally the maternity ward tends to be feminine. Everywhere you look are flowers and frilly nighties and exposed breasts. This makes some men feel awkward. Nothing wrong with that. How would a woman feel at a working men's club, full of blokes covered in brick dust, drinking ale and talking football? Perfectly at ease these days. The modern woman can retain full feminine identity while quaffing pints and making rude gestures at the referee. 'Who's the wanker in last year's black?'

Eddie Izzard is correct. The same rule doesn't apply to twenty-first century man. Attire him with short skirt and park a port and lemon in his meaty hand, then have him perch on a bar stool perusing a copy of *Colour Me Beautiful*. What sort of man do you have? In Camden Passage they'd still accuse him of being a caveman, but anywhere north of N1 and he'd be modelling several ugly shades of black and blue.

The maternity ward is a woman's domain. The patients are all women, the staff are mostly women, even most of the visitors are female. You know they want you to feel welcome but you can't help feeling a bit uncomfortable.

While your partner was a resident, you were a mere visitor, however frequent. Little things may have irked: nearest gents' toilet was a couple of flights upstairs; mum was always the one shown how to care for baby; dads were not allowed tea from the trolley.

For the first few days of fatherhood you felt just a teensy bit of an interloper. Once you stooped to pick the remains of a fig roll from your shoe and were curtly informed that biscuits were for 'patients only'. And not once did anyone offer to check your sanitary pad.

Not that your partner was having the time of her life. She couldn't wait to get out of the institution. You feel likewise. Once you are all home you can start to be a real dad and mum. You can only truly grow into the role of parenting when you have control over all the decisions.

That's Gross Man

Certain preparations need to be made. Firstly, the home must be scrupulously clean and tidy. Yes, that includes doing the washing up. Also mopping up the living-room carpet where you puked up after the head-wetting session. It's true to say no matter how meticulous you are, though, the house will never satisfy. Five days of bachelor living have let the genie out of the bottle.

Who lives in a house like this? Let's examine the evidence with our expert . . .

'At first impression, this person does not drink. There is not one bottle of wine in the wine rack. But a simple check outside the back door reveals dozens of empties. He appears to have his own bottle bank. A sign says the council pick up Mondays and Thursdays . . . and Saturdays . . . and twice on Sundays.

'Back in the kitchen we discover this householder is a minimalist eater. Fridge contents: a tub of I Can't Believe It's Not Butter, half a tin of curry paste and twenty Benson and Hedges. Wait a minute, there is a cardboard box containing two slices of pepperoni pizza and an ash tray. So that's twenty Benson and Hedges and couple of very long stubs.

'Over to the, er, library area we find a copy of the Carlsberg Lager book of Association Football and next to it a companion volume of the Association Football book of Drinking Carlsberg . . . Other books include . . . No, that's the lot.

'In the living room we find this attractive sofa with its matching low-tog, daytime-use, duvet. Splayed out on the carpet just in front are the remote controls. Twelve of them, including the usual TV, video, hi-fi, etc. etc., but one seems to be an infra-red corkscrew. And another . . . (sound effects: toilet flushing) Well, that really is high-tech. Over to you, David . . .'

Ten-point Plan For Homecoming
1 Fill the house with flowers. All right, a couple of bunches. Even though half of Holland is beside the hospital bed, it won't hurt to buy a few more. It's really important that there is at least one bunch from you.
2 Check the larder for essential provisions: bread, milk etc.
3 Buy enough food to last a couple of days.
4 Spray air freshener around the place. If you smoke, get windows open to ventilate the place. Babies don't like smoke.
5 Get the cot or crib set up in the bedroom. Rig up a mobile on the frame. (No, not a mobile phone, a mobile with planes and balloons on bits of string.)
6 Tidy up.
7 Shove some washing in the machine. It's that thing in the kitchen that looks like a telly.
8 Put some wine in the rack. Set some fizz chilling in the fridge.
9 The absolute killer. Get around to some job she's been nagging you to do for months, like putting the shower curtain back up, or fixing that hinge on the kitchen cupboard.
10 Get your mum round to help. You won't get half of it done on your own. When your mum gets round, tell her you have to pop out for the flowers and let her do most of it.

The Pick Up

No doubt you will be provided with a huge list of things to bring to hospital when picking up your new family: a particular coat for her, a specific blanket to wrap the baby in, etc. etc. etc. Robbing Fort Knox wouldn't take this much planning.

You must also find time to fit a baby seat in the car. Most modern ones are removable. There are several on the market ranging from about £25 to over £150. What accounts for the price difference is hard to say. Surely they are all safe. Unless for the top of range £150 you walk away without a scratch, but some of the cheaper models only carry a 'minor maiming' guarantee. You'll have to check with the sales assistant.

'Look, pal, I'm not interested in the safety aspects. I want extra features. I want a drinks holder, a compass, remote CD changing and a microphone so he can talk to the driver. I also want red leather with chrome buckles. And he's a very broad baby so I'll need the Nigel Mansell model.'

Finding somewhere to park the car outside the hospital needs some thought. Not only are there triple yellow lines and red zones, but they've now put up signs threatening to clamp anyone who quite sensibly ignores them. There's even a jobsworth security guard in flannel suit and ray-bans patrolling the area. You know the type.

'No, sir. You cannot leave your vehicle here.'

He has the demeanour of ex-CIA, fresh from supplying AK47s to the Contras. More likely he's ex-B&Q and the nearest he's got to action is rugby tackling an old age pensioner who forgot to pay for a bottle of Superglue.

'I'll only be a minute.'

'I'm sorry, sir. You cannot park your vehicle here.'

'How come all these vehicles can park here?'

'They are ambulances, sir.'

'So?'

'I'm sorry, sir.'

'You're not sorry. Not a bit sorry. If you're so sorry, why aren't you down on your knees crying? Come on, I want to see you beg, you bastard . . . Will a couple of quid cover it?'

'Adequately, sir. Would you like it valeted for an extra three pounds?'

The Getaway

So many firsts and now another one. Your baby's first car journey. Also your first experience driving with a baby in the car. Thankfully the trip was completely uneventful. Apart from the crash.

It started when the baby got sick, and a stream of hot just-imbibed breast milk sprayed out from the back seat and hit you on the back of the neck. You reacted as you thought you should by flooring the accelerator. The quicker you could get home the better.

Your partner screamed at you to stop the car. You would have, too, if the police hadn't been right behind you. Stopping suddenly would have seemed suspicious, what with the MOT having run out and the number plate. By bunching up a couple of letters and the strategic placement of a few black screws you managed to make B194 RGM read BIG PENIS GRUNT MACHINE.

Instead of stopping you swung a hard left down a back double. The one with the speed bumps.

'If I can just get it up to 38 miles an hour, we'll skip right over them.'

Okay, the baby sort of, kind of, slightly slipped out of the baby chair. But just a little bit. There was no need for your partner to scream like that. If she hadn't, you wouldn't have stopped so quickly. And then the police car wouldn't have hit you up the rear end. Obviously they hadn't heeded the sign on the back window: 'Keep Back – Baby On Board.'

A Saucer of Milk

For the first week you have your baby home, the sensation you feel most is probably fear. Certainly you feel joy and amazement, but you are anxious that in your not very capable hands your baby will die. Whose idea was it to land you with a newborn human to look after? For all you knew about them, they might as well have parked a baby giraffe in the front room, or baby duck-billed platypus.

Your fear may stem from the time as a child that you brought a sick hedgehog home. You did everything you could for it. You kept it warm, fed it, quenched its thirst. More than anything you loved that hedgehog more than you realised you could love anything. Four hours later the damn thing went and died on you.

Well, babies are not hedgehogs. Babies are mini versions of you. They need to be kept a bit warmer than you, and they only drink milk. But basically their sensations are similar to yours. You can apply what you might want to what they might want. Common sense doesn't work with hedgehogs because you have very little in common with them. A hedgehog might need to be kept in the freezer to feel comfortable. It may need a three-course meal every twenty minutes. You don't know. I don't know. (This isn't a hedgehog guide: *You're a Spiky Mammal Trying to Cross the M25 Too, Mate!*)

Unless your baby is already very ill, common sense is all you need to look after it. Advice from friends, family, health visitors and guide books help put your mind at rest, but without any of them you'd still be all right.

Main Fears With Your New Baby

My baby keeps crying. It must be dying.
Unlikely. Terminally sick babies do not cry much because they don't have the strength. The baby probably is hungry, or tired,

or needs its nappy changed. But what if you've tried all that and the baby still cries? Most likely the baby is unsettled after a difficult birth, or was just more comfortable in mummy's tummy.

My baby sleeps all the time. It must be dying.
Unlikely. Newborn babies often sleep almost constantly for the first couple of weeks.

My baby never sleeps. It must be dying.
Unlikely. Some newborn babies sleep very little.

My baby might freeze to death in the night.
Unlikely. Touch the baby's forehead. If it feels cold add a blanket or a cardigan. If the heads feels very hot, take one off.

My baby might die of cot death.
Unlikely. Be aware of the precautions but do not unduly worry. Cot death is very rare, occurring in about 0.2 per cent of all babies born. To put it another way, if your partner had a baby every year for five hundred years, one of them might die of cot death.

The current safety guidelines for cot death avoidance are:
1 Put your baby to sleep on its back.
2 Don't give it a pillow.
3 Use a ventilated mattress.
4 Don't smoke in the same building.

Ring of Confidence

A couple of days after getting home you barge into the bedroom and find your partner puffing into an inflatable rubber ring. (For one dreadful moment you thought she had finally discovered Blow Up Bernice who lives in the cupboard under the stairs.)
    'Bit chilly for the seaside, isn't it?'
    'No, it's for my . . . you know.'
    'No. Remind me.'
    'So I can sit down.'
    'A pillow for your bad back, eh? Well, my holistic physician reckons the best cure for that is plenty of ferocious rumpy-pumpy.'
    Your trousers are already at your ankles.
    'Not my back.'

'Aah, I get it.'

And you do. As your erection subsides you begin to wonder what the current condition of your partner's vagina is exactly. Is it roadworthy, just about running, or ready for the breaker's yard? The last time you carried out an inspection it had just suffered a major prang. A doctor was performing emergency repairs with the medical equivalent of visor and oxyacetylene torch. Heroic stuff, but to your untutored eye it looked like a write-off.

Breaking for parts. Late model Vagina Coupé. Many panels undamaged; recently replaced cervix; low-mileage clitoris. Two hundred pounds the lot, or swap for Sony PlayStation.

Most tears and episiotomies (surgical cuts) during delivery are minor, affecting only the outer layers of the vagina and labia. Occasionally the muscles underneath are injured too. The stitching helps the natural repair along. Depending on the extent of damage it may take many months before your partner is sufficiently recovered to make love. The stitches are dissolvable so there's no need to have them removed.

Clearly any bruising and tearing will cause your partner quite a bit of pain, hence the rubber ring to sit on. Other soothing treatments will include herbal baths, salt-water washing and ice-packs. It's not a black eye so don't come home with two pounds of (Reduced: Eat Today) rump steak.

The startling amount of stretching your partner's sexual organ underwent may also have concerned you. Be reassured the vagina is very elastic and should quickly contract back to its normal size. There is no danger of her becoming the proverbial 'Albert Hall'. Unfortunately, your own proverbial 'Woodbine' will still be a sad, skinny offering, even sadder for its perpetual and repeated hand-rolling.

Make Mine a Double

There's something fascinating about breast feeding. How is it possible that a couple of bags of flesh, very attractive ones, granted, can miraculously become the suppliers of every nutritional need? It's like waking up one morning and discovering your buttocks have become side-by-side branches of Budgen and Kwik-Save. Rather unnerving for you. And what about the bloke who stands between the two shops selling the *Big Issue*? Boy, is he in for a shock.

Why should it seem strange that breasts make milk? As an experiment you ask a five year old where milk comes from and he replies: 'The kitchen fridge.' You chortle patronisingly and inform the poor dim child that although he gets it from the kitchen fridge, milk originates from the really big fridges at the supermarket.

Somehow we have forgotten where cows' milk comes from. (The clue is in the question.) We sort of imagine milk is manufactured out at some huge smoke-billowing factory in Sheffield's green belt. But once reminded, it's obvious that if silly old moos can make milk, gallons of it every day, just standing around chewing grass, why shouldn't your partner. Not that such a comparison will endear her to you. On no account attempt to improve production by slinging a couple of heavy bells around her neck and sitting the baby on a three-legged stool.

Milk is produced in tiny bunches of grape-like structures called alveoli in her breasts. The sucking action of the baby stimulates her pituitary gland near her brain. This gland sends a hormone to her breasts which instructs them to make milk, lots of it, and hurry up!

All the constituent parts of milk are in the bloodstream. In fact breast milk is quite similar to blood but without the red blood cells. A vegetarian vampire might feed on breast milk.

Another amazing thing about breast milk is that it is both constant and self-replenishing. This brings to mind the old joke about a stupid man who likes to drink a lot (in less enlightened days he would have been Irish but he is now merely described as a net beneficiary of the European budget) and is granted two wishes. For the first wish he asks for a never-ending pint of Guinness. He drinks it down, then says, 'That was great. I'll have another one of those.'

Which begs the question, why have two breasts? Why not just have one? A really big one in the middle. A superbreast. A huge awe-inspiring singleton dangling from the centre of the chest with a six-inch-wide cyclopic nipple.

Actually, it wouldn't even need to be big. Small breasts and small nipples apparently produce plenty of milk equally well. The bloke could have ordered a never-ending half of Guinness.

Milk travels from the alveoli through little ducts to the tiny holes in the nipple where it sprays out in a fine jet to the baby's mouth. This milk-injection system means there's no need for a horrible disfiguring carburettor between the boobs. Although, it's true some men might actually find this a turn-on.

The requirement for two breasts might be explained by the wear and tear on the outlet jets. The baby's relentless sucking

can result in nipple soreness and cracking, which are the main reasons why a lot of women give up.

Virtually everyone in medical circles is mad keen for women to solely breast feed, at least for the first few weeks. Formula milks, made from cows' milk, have been 'humanised' to approximate breast milk, but don't contain all the same nutrients as breast milk. More importantly, formula milk feeding does not give the child the benefits of its mother's immune system.

In the sixties they told mothers bottle was best. Now it's 'breast is best' for the baby. In another generation it may be something different. Despite the bewildering array of advice, women are statistically proven to follow it to the letter while in hospital, after which they stick two fingers up to the quacks and boffins and do what feels right for them.

Baby Blues

> Woke up this morning
> Crying baby in my hand
> My boobs are like udders
> And my love equipment is all shot to pieces.

Bo Diddley never sang that song. Neither did his twin sister, La Toya Diddley. Possibly because it's crap but also because post-natal depression is something not many have wanted to sing about.

Childbirth has hardly advertised the problem either. Our images of a newborn baby are all hearts and flowers, boundless love and joy. No woman says:

'Having children was the best thing that ever happened to me, apart from the six months of manic depression I felt afterwards. Mind you, the straitjacket they gave me was terribly flattering; bit tight across the bust but very supportive of the tummy area. It's true there was some initial embarrassment wearing it outside the house but I told people it was the latest Alistair McQueen. Most commented it was nice to see designers making halfway wearable clothes for a change.'

Despite this, the baby blues is quite common in women to varying degrees. It can also occur in men. (Don't worry, you get your five minutes of fame in the next section.)

Where these feelings spring from is a complex area. Not that one has to look far for ideas:

- Physical injuries of childbirth
- Hormonal changes after giving birth
- New and constant demands of motherhood
- All-consuming exhaustion while trying to cope
- Lack of sleep from a crying baby
- Feelings of guilt from failure to bond with the baby
- Fear her life is over because she's stuck with a crying baby

Exactly. Post-natal depression seems the sensible option when faced with that lot. Most men can get depressed because their best mate has a better company car than them; or because their favourite football team has taken on a really stupid sponsor.

Most women don't suffer from severe depression after giving birth. The general experience is a few days of incredible highs immediately after the birth followed by a couple of days of let down, then back to normal.

The main difficulty with prolonged post-natal depression is if your partner doesn't realise she has it. She probably thinks she is just exhausted and not fully recovered. Luckily she has a warm, sensitive, caring partner in tune with the minute fluctuations of her emotions. Consequently you respond in the following ways:

'It's four o'clock in the afternoon. I bet Kate Adie's not still in her nightie.'

'It was great down the pub last night. All your mates were down there, drinking, dancing and on the pull.'

'I'm thinking of inventing a bandage you can pee through.'

'Stop crying. I can't hear the commentary.'

Dealing with the blues is not easy. People don't want to face up to depression. Probably because the subject is, well, so bloody depressing.

The solution to depression is to think positively. Which is about as helpful as saying the solution to being poor is to become a millionaire.

What you can do for your partner:

- Recognise she may be depressed

- Help as much as you can with the baby

- Take leave from work. You are entitled to it (unpaid – thanks a lot, Tony)

- Don't expect her to be the instant perfect mum

- Get her to join mum and toddler groups

- Help with housework

- Talk about how you are both feeling

In addition try some of these supportive phrases:

'You're right. Day clothes are a waste of money. What tie goes with these pyjamas?'

'Your old mate Debbie was down the pub last night, looking sad and pissed up in the arms of some squaddie. Apparently she has the clap so bad she'll never have kids.'

'I've invented a bandage you can pee through.'

'John Barnes is such a useless summariser I feel like crying myself.'

Or maybe don't.

Daddy Blues

> Woke up this morning
> Penis in my hand.
> Wife says you can put that away
> Her love equipment is all shot to pieces.

It is a real song. It is. Really. Have you ever been to the French Quarter in New Orleans? So how do you know? . . . Well, it should have been.

Men get post-natal depression too. Rarely is it severe, but many can feel a bit flat. The reasons for this are as follows:

- Overwhelmed by the financial responsibilities of fatherhood
- Feel you can't go out. End of your freedom
- Sick of coping with first pregnant and now poorly partner
- No support from your mates or employers
- Treated as second-class citizen at the hospital
- Feel clumsy around the baby
- Emotional rollercoaster of the birth
- You look at the baby and you feel nothing
- You, the man, are supposed to be the coping, strong one
- No sex

See, that's ten reasons why you might feel depressed. Your partner only had seven. It must be much worse for you. If us blokes have got to cope with namby-pamby stuff like depression we're going to be damned good at it.

Top Tips . . . Depression To Win!
1 If she's not dressed by teatime, you won't get dressed ever. Take all your day clothes from the closet and fling them out of the window. (If you live in a ground-floor flat, ask the people upstairs if you can borrow one of their windows.)
2 Buy a boxed set of Leonard Cohen CDs. (Do not attempt to listen to them.)
3 Wear only black pyjamas. (But beware of embarrassing staining.)
4 Refuse to eat ever again. (If after half an hour you get a bit peckish, go out and buy a whole box of Doritos and say you'll eat the lot if you bloody well feel like it.)
5 Refuse ever to go to work again. (Warning: this may affect your right to benefits. When signing on, affect a jovial tone and say you'd be happy to work for £2.20 an hour but the phrase 'Would you like fries with that, sir?' is completely beyond your capabilities.)

For most people the realisation that they actually are a bit depressed is enough to start to feel better. Once you have properly analysed the reasons behind it, you might well decide things aren't so bad.

Prolonged depression is, of course, a serious illness affecting your ability to function and make any rational decisions. Either see a doctor and get some pills, or buy a book that shows you how to break out of it.

Most importantly do not try to cope in silence alone. Do not start thinking nobody cares and you are just being an irritating nuisance. (But this is exactly the kind of irrational thinking depressed people fall into.)

Cheerful Note

The danger behind pointing out some of the potential pitfalls of having a child is giving the impression that all the news is bad. Her depression, your depression, cracked nipples, and what about all that cleaning and running around you are supposed to do. Let's concentrate on a few positives.

You are a dad. You have achieved parenthood. Which can't be bad. You've heard about folk becoming obsessed with becoming parents to the point where they take out second mortgages to pay for medical treatment. For you it came easily and naturally. You must have saved thousands.

You feel an instantaneous bond with your child. And you don't mind saying you've earned it. You read this book. You followed the pregnancy every step of the way. (Each and every one. You've got thicker thighs than a lighthouse keeper.) And when it came to the birth, let's just say you were the one single person in the room who was totally indispensable . . . apart from your partner, obviously . . . and the midwives and the anaesthetist . . . Whatever. You're happy to receive any awards on behalf of the team.

You feel really grown up. Settling down with a long-term partner and having children must be the most grown-up thing you can do. It's equivalent to buying your first pint or seeing your first 18 film. You didn't even have to lie about your age for this one. You only had to lie about your weight and your job prospects and how much you spend each week on drink and . . .

9

First Weeks: It's Just a Sixteen-year Phase

Lessons in Love

As the first few weeks go on you realise you can cope with a baby. The basics are picked up in a few days. There's nothing like having to do a job for twenty-four hours a day to give you rapid experience and expertise.

If you tot up all the golf lessons you've ever had, the chances are it won't add up to the time you spend looking after a baby in one day. No wonder you've learned quicker. Obviously, golf is much harder. You aren't likely to suffer from the yips when changing a nappy, causing you to lip out of your child's genital area and carve your wet wipe halfway up his back. Rocking a baby in your arms is far easier to master that swinging a titanium-headed long-shafted hollow-backed Bulky Bob. Even Nick Faldo could do rock-a-bye baby without missing the cut. Even Greg Norman wouldn't choke . . . I think the point has been made.

More Reality, Less Bites

As a new father you'll be so enamoured with your little tot you won't be able to wait to get home from work to see him. The thought of going across to the pub for a quick pint is anathema to you. (Don't sell your tankard. This phase lasts three weeks – tops.)

Your friends and colleagues may just have to get used to the new you; drinking less, smoking less . . . erm, eating a bit more actually, but you are taking less bites to consume an entire Big Mac. Inside you feel happier and more in tune with the things that really matter in life.

Everywhere you go people want to share in your joy as new parents. And they do. Your baby feels almost like public property. Complete strangers feel at liberty to stare at him, make faces at him, poke and prod him. Like that woman in the Post Office queue.

'Oh, he's lovely . . . How many weeks is he? Such a chubby little face . . . Just like his father . . . I bet they both like their food . . . Ooh, he's done a little burp. I bet his dad does that too . . . How are your stitches, dear? Have you tried live yoghurt?'

Mostly this is other women talking to your partner. You get to stand around like a big lug, shifting from foot to foot and wishing the old bag would mind her own business. How would she like you to be so personal?

'Oh, that's a nice shopping trolley . . . Spanish leather, is it? Or did you carve some of the excess skin from your neck?'

Baby Care: the Basics

The rigmarole of catering for all the needs of your baby seems quite a palaver at first glance. But it quickly becomes a simple routine. You'll get the hang of it, speed up and cut out the superfluous.

Nappies
For example, the first couple of weeks you'll change a nappy using the entire contents of your bulging nappy bag, exactly as they showed you in hospital. Your basic kit is something like this:
1 Clean nappy – and spares in case you make a mess of it.
2 Balls of cotton wool – to clean pooh off.
3 Bowl of tepid water – to dip cotton wool into.
4 Towel – to dry baby's bum.
5 Talc – to get bum really dry.
6 Box of wet wipes – second clean to get in crevices.
7 Zinc barrier cream – to protect from nappy rash.
8 Antiseptic cream – to treat nappy rash.
9 Kitchen roll – to clean up excess water from cleaning.
10 Nappy bags – to put dirty nappy in.

11 Toy to keep baby occupied – because all this takes so ruddy long.

As you work through the contents of this bag, you end up muddling the order so the talc gets mixed in the cream and goes lumpy. Next, your baby gets bored with the toy and grabs the bowl of water, and the box of wipes ends up wrapped inside the dirty nappy. The whole caboodle takes about twenty-five minutes. If you've turned away from the snooker, Ronnie O'Sullivan has made a couple of hundred breaks, three more half centuries and has won the match five nil. You missed the whole thing.

Within a month this kit will have been pared down to:

1 Clean nappy – one.
2 Wet wipe – one. (You are now so dextrous with a wet wipe you can with a single swipe eradicate the world's worst diarrhoea from bum, thighs, genitals, bellybutton and back.
3 Tub of cream – one (combined barrier/antiseptic cream e.g. Sudocream).

You have turned nappy changing into a PlayStation game. Rip-rip. Swish. Dab. Up and over. Tape-tape. Done.

The entire process takes twenty-nine seconds. Your baby's bum never touched the changing mat and Terry Griffiths hasn't even finished chalking his cue.

Formula for success
Making up a feed for your baby is straightforward. You merely turn to your partner and say you'll give the baby the bottle if she goes downstairs, prepares bottle and brings it back up to the bedroom – preferably with a cup of tea for you. She replies: isn't it about time you learned how to make the bottle up yourself? You retort: you replaced the driver's side wiper on her car last weekend. How come she's never learned to do that! She comes back with: you are the one who wanted to use the car. You are also the one who broke the old wiper off in a fit of rage because you snagged your hand on it while cleaning the car. And the new wiper still doesn't work anyhow because you knackered the whole mechanism. Undaunted, you land the killer blow: would she like some toast with her cup of tea?

This does the trick. You pad down to the kitchen wondering how in God's name one makes up a bottle feed. She's always going on about how you should have learned by now. But the baby is only seven weeks old. He's only had what . . . two, four, six . . . about three hundred and fifty feeds. You suppose that's quite a few. Perhaps you should get round to it.

Better idea. Your partner normally keeps a couple of spare feeds ready made up in the fridge. Use one of those.

Nothing. All gone. As you slam the fridge door in disgust, a raucous cackle emits from the bedroom. She's planned this whole thing. Right, then, you'll show her. One perfectly made bottle coming up.

Hang on, though, maybe she's hidden them in the freezer. In a few seconds the kitchen lino is strewn with frozen chops, ready meals, packets of pitta bread. It looks like someone has ram-raided a branch of Iceland. However, ready made-up bottles are nowhere to be seen.

Another mad cackle comes from the bedroom. Bitch. She's enjoying this. You've a good mind to spit in her tea. Or stir it with your penis. Might be a bit hot, though, unless you cooled the tea first, then stirred it with your willy, then heated it up again in the microwave . . .

Surely learning to make up a bottle is easier. All the instructions are on the back of the tin.

How to make up a bottle

You fill a sterilised bottle with the required amount of pre-boiled water e.g. five ounces. Then add required number of scoops of the formula milk. If it's five ounces, it'll be five scoops. Shake. Heat in microwave (but *always* shake afterwards) or bowl of hot water. (Or if you add boiling water, cool in a bowl of cold water.) Test temperature on your wrist and insert teat into baby's mouth.

If you want to get clever, you can use half boiling and half pre-boiled water so as to achieve approximately the right temperature double quick. If baby is screaming for a feed, even double quick will feel plenty long enough.

All utensils used for a baby need to be well cleaned and sterilised (e.g. bottles, teats, spoons, jugs). Sterilisation tablets can be bought and dropped into a bowl of ordinary water. You just leave all the clean stuff in there till you need it. Alternatively, there are electric steam sterilisers on the market for about thirty pounds.

Feeding

The invention of bottle feeding must be the single biggest advance in the sharing of baby care between mother and father.

Instinctively a baby loves most whoever feeds it. Rottweiler owners know the same thing. In return they can expect loyalty and absolute protection. You could try putting a sticker of a snarling baby in your front window above the words 'Watch it! I live here'. For maximum burglary deterrent effect, it may be best to wait until a couple of teeth come through.

Giving your baby his bottle is a nice thing to do. The baby lies there cradled in your arms, enjoying sucking away, grateful eyes staring back at you. Babies can't cry while they are sucking a bottle. Neither do they want to. Drinking a pleasant-tasting liquid seems to calm his every discomfort or anxiety. Remind you of anyone?

After a large and satisfying feed, your baby gives all the appearance of being drunk. His eyes droop, his head lolls and dribbles of unswallowed liquid run down his chin. Remind you of anyone?

Some babies love drinking milk so much they will continue to consume it long after they have had enough. They drink a bottle, vomit most of it down your back, drink some more, throw that up, and still cry for more. Eventually you have to say, 'I'm sorry, sonny. But I think you've had enough for one night.' Surely, no one's ever said that to you.

Winding
Winding your baby after a big feed is certainly the most satisfying part. From the days when you were a small boy you've known burping was tremendous fun. Quite why girls have never shared this enthusiasm has always been a mystery. At the supermarket, why help Mummy put the food on the conveyor belt like your sister did, when you can get the attention of a whole shop just by letting rip with a near-popping bull-froginous parp.

One particularly wet and interminable spring term was passed by seeing who could complete the most mini-burps in a minute.

'Erp!'
'Forty-one.'
'Erp!'
'Forty-two.'
'Oieek!'
'Forty-three – No, forty-two still. That one didn't count.'
'Erp! Yes, it bloody did. Erp! I've just got the – Oieek! – hiccups.'

Now, not only can you burp for Britain yourself, but you

have the chance to groom a successor, who, with the right preparation, might one day become heir to your burp-in-a-minute title.

'This is a very proud moment. I want to thank my father, who trained me up since I was a baby . . . I want any youngsters watching to know I'm a clean burp-athlete. So say no to performance-enhancing fizzy drinks.'

How to burp your baby

Winding is achieved by simply holding the baby upright at your shoulder. You can lightly rub or pat his back. In a few moments he should let out a satisfying croak and be ready to finish his feed.

Feel free to compliment your child for loudness and depth of belch. Unlike adult burping this is not considered rude but a cause for wide celebration. Repeating the name 'Bishop of Canterbury' (as in Arch!) after every emission may be taking things too far.

Crying

Is the Pope a Catholic? Very likely. Although there were rumours that he was willing to become Chief Rabbi unless they upped his money.

Does a bear shit in the woods? Probably. Unless it's a particularly hygienic bear who has employed a plumber to put in a reinforced toilet, then got in several rolls of Wide-Boy 'quad-quilted' loo rolls and is prepared to spend several hours of valuable roaring time removing the extensive Klingon problem from his hirsute behind.

Do babies cry? Yes.

It is estimated they do so for on average three hours out of every twenty-four. This is a lot of crying for one day. You probably haven't cried for a grand total of a hundred and eighty minutes since you were ten. Think about it. There was the time the dog got run over, the time you got nicked for bunking the tube, and every time you watched an episode of *100 Great Sporting Moments*.

Babies cry so much because they have no useful form of action. If they feel cold in the night, they can't grab a couple of dressing gowns from the back of the door and spread them on top of the duvet. When hungry, they cannot go to the fridge. When they are bored, there is no kicking the skirting board for half an hour until your partner says, 'Oh, go to the bloody pub if you need to that much.'

A Checklist For Crying

- Hunger? – Just been fed. Tried more, threw it up. Go to next.

- Cold? – Can't be. You are roasting hot. Go to next.

- Dirty nappy? – Nothing lurking in there. Not wet. Go to next.

- Bored? – Throws every toy away. Yanked the mobile from its moorings and chucked it out of the cot. Go to next.

- Frightened? – What of? Go to next.

- Uncomfortable? – You paid sixty quid for that day chair. Go to next.

- Tired and irritable? – Aren't we all. Why don't you go to sleep then? Go to next.

- Having a nightmare about being born? – Eh? Yes, there is a theory that . . . forget it. Go to next.

- Colic? – Could be. Cries in the evenings. Screams frantically. But the gripe water did nothing. (These days they have no alcohol in them which makes them safer but less effective.) Tried the doctor but she says the drugs they used to use are not considered safe any more.

- Needs comfort? – Picked the baby up, rocked him gently, he stops crying. Bingo! Put him down he starts again. Fine, so you've discovered how to make the baby stop but it means you can't do anything else, including getting some sleep.

For whatever reason babies start to cry, by the time you discover the reason and satisfy their need, they are often so worked up they can't stop crying. If picking your baby up doesn't work, you can try certain 'tricks' to distract them, e.g. running the kitchen tap, singing, turning the TV or radio to white noise. Otherwise, a walk up the road in the buggy nearly always helps. As a last resort, try taking them out in the car for a drive.

Mr Angry

We've all read horrific stories about parents battering their babies. We've wondered how on earth they could possibly hit a tiny defenceless baby. After spending a few weeks living with a relentlessly crying baby and not getting much sleep, we know how. The temptation to try to shut them up with a smattering of violence is there in all of us. Fortunately, most of us restrain ourselves, although at times it's mighty close.

When the demons rise up remind yourself of the following points:

1 A smack won't do the trick. The baby will cry more. Only by really hurting a baby could you stop it crying, which clearly is not your intention.

2 A smack won't make you feel better either. It'll make you feel guilty and worse.

3 Shaking or hitting babies is very dangerous. Despite the robustness of their cries, babies are very fragile.

4 If things get really bad get someone to give you a break for half an hour. During that time it's important to get right away from the crying baby, i.e. out of the house. You'll come back refreshed.

5 If no one is around to help, give yourself a break. Put the baby safely in its cot, shut the door and pour yourself a small glass of wine. Promise yourself a really large glass of wine when your partner gets back. You could try phoning a friend. Whingeing is hugely underrated as a stress reliever.

Sleeper

You've spent the last twenty odd years of your life sleeping too much. Weekend lie-ins till midday, snoozes on the couch, forty winks on your towel in the garden. After a really late night you've even tried sleeping in the toilet cubicle at work but could never quite get your elbow comfortable on the toilet roll holder.

And in the car, of course. Even out on the road you've got to have your Power Snooze, haven't you? There's a spot just off the main road where you go to pick up office supplies; nice little cul-de-sac, shaded by trees, no through traffic. Then it's jacket up at the window to keep the light out, blow-up pillow out of the briefcase, set the alarm on your mobile phone, stretch out across the back seat and away you go to dreamland. Those car sleeps may lack something in comfort but are so much sweeter for the knowledge you are being paid by the hour.

Actually you've always been a good sleeper.

'I can sleep anywhere, me. I could sleep on the branch of a tree. Long as I'm warm, I could kip on the roof of the Empire State Building. No kidding. Strap me to the wing of an aeroplane at thirty thousand feet, a supersonic aeroplane, right . . . so I'm on the wing of Concordski, the Russian version was noisier, and it's raining hard, and the plane is in a steep dive, probably crashing. But me, slip me under my duvet, and I'm out like a light. No probs.'

You like sleeping. It's good for you. Maybe you've wasted a bit too much time in the Land of Nod, and if you had a minute back for every hour you've slept . . . no, there's nothing you'd rather have done.

Now it looks like pay-back time.

You've heard about people with good babies. Ones that sleep through the night from the first week onwards. Your baby is not a good baby. Your baby would do well to sleep through a weather bulletin. Granted weather bulletins last a bit longer at four in the morning because TV time is cheap but, blimey, it's four in the morning! You saw the three o'clock bulletin too. It doesn't matter that it's going to be dry and fine with highs of 23 degrees tomorrow because you're going to spend the whole day with the curtains drawn trying to catch up on your sleep.

Your baby has this trick. He sleeps all the time when you're out shopping, pushing him along in his buggy. Same thing when he's in his little car seat and you're driving him somewhere. He seems to have worked out that if you are doing either of these things you cannot be sleeping too. How he works this out you are not sure.

Your baby has another trick. Most evenings he might have a little snooze about ten o'clock. This is a welcome relief because you want to watch telly for a while, wind down, indulge in a little freelance vintage-checking. About half eleven you go up to the bedroom to get an early night. You creep into the room, having already undressed in the hall so as not to wake the baby. You pick your way across the carpet avoiding all the creaking floor-boards and peek into the crib, hardly daring to blink, let alone breathe. Fine: fast asleep.

You make your way to your own bed. There's a really tricky section where you have to hurdle a wide group of squeaky boards and bound almost silently on to the bed. Some hours earlier you already turned back the duvet to make even that quieter. Having made it, you allow yourself a small sigh of relief. You turn to see your partner creeping into the room to perform the same routine. You gesticulate violently to her not to bother looking in the crib. She does anyway, but makes it safely over to her side of the bed. She slips under the covers as smoothly as a snake in a James Bond movie.

You smile at each other. You mouth goodnight. You release the tension in your neck. Your head falls lightly on the pillow.

'Aaargh!'

Your head snaps up, heart both sinking and beating at a thousand miles per hour. Oh, please no. But the baby stops crying. You listen intently. You hear a bit of snuffling, but no more crying. You relax your neck muscles and the moment your ear touches the pillow again –

'AAAARRRGH! ARRGGH!'

Oh, for God's sake. How does the baby know? And why does he see fit to torture you like this? He had plenty of opportunities to set off earlier but had to wait until you were about to go to sleep.

'I'll go,' says your partner.

'No, I'll go. You went last night,' you say wearily.

'So did you. And it was the awful three-till-five a.m. shift.'

'Yeah, I know. That's why I want to do the early one. You can do the three-till-five.'

So you pick up your screaming bundle of love and carry him to the living room to begin counting isobars.

The very worst thing about lack of sleep is that it leaves you totally unable to cope. For new parents, looking after a baby can be a rather testing time, particularly in the patience stakes. Few people are very patient when they've had less down time than Warren Beatty's todger.

Fixation

Sleep becomes your magnificent obsession. You are the Van Gogh of shut-eye and the Beethoven of kip. Your fixation with sleep is total and uncompromising. You live, breathe, eat and drink sleep. The only thing you don't do is *sleep* sleep.

Woe betide anyone foolish enough to ask you a simple question such as 'Sleep okay, last night?' You will launch into a three-hour diatribe, minutely detailing the catalogue of disturbances and rest patterns through the nocturnal hours. Your relentless pacing of the house with crying baby at your shoulder. Your fevered attempts to settle and soothe. Your battle with the evil demons tempting you to throttle your own baby in pursuit of a few hours of wonderful, treasured, beautiful, undisturbed sleep . . . No, no, 'sleep' is too tinny and insignificant a word for it. What you need is blessed, undisturbed, baritone-deep and dead-to-the-world slumber.

The days when the most exciting thing you did in the night was splash your slippers with urine are long gone. Every night is *Hamlet* and *Macbeth* rolled into one. And that Kenneth Branagh never could write anyway.

Solutions

A newborn baby will normally sleep for 12 to 14 hours out of 24. Which sounds fine but the patterns will not be as regular as yours. The most you can expect is about five hours at a stretch and only one of this length. The rest will be broken into shorter bursts. They do not know the difference between night and day.

The good news is four out of five babies will sleep through the night by the time they are a year old. Which means you only have to go three hundred and sixty-five consecutive nights without proper sleep. That's a breeze. Think of the other twenty per cent of parents. They'll be staggering around with eyes like a giant panda's for much longer. (My first baby hardly slept for 18 months.)

Tips for getting your baby through the night:

- Keep him warm (but not too warm) and in the dark.

- Restrict sleep in the evenings.

- Give good feed just before bed.

- Change nappy before bed. Don't change nappy in the night.

- Let him have a dummy. (Of my three kids, only one had a dummy and only one slept well. The same one.)

- If he wakes, lift into bed with you.

- If he is on both formula and breast milk, the 'heavier' formula milk tends to satisfy them for longer. So you could try making the last feed before bed a bottle feed. (If your baby is solely breast fed, don't think this lets you off the hook. Some clown invented a thing called a breast pump, allowing the stuff to be decanted into a bottle and given to the baby by anyone. During the night this 'anyone' is you.)

- Try to get him into a regular routine at bedtime – 'Play time, bath time, feed time and BED time. Get the message!' No, he doesn't. These routines have to be persevered with.

Many diet plans (or other self-help books) guarantee to help you lose weight . . . 'Or your money back!' *You're Pregnant Too, Mate!* makes no such promise on its advice.

Two reasons:

Firstly, those guarantees always come with the rider that you must follow the diet for at least four weeks *to the letter*. And you don't. You always end up supplementing one of the 'nutritious shakes' for egg, bacon, sausage and chips. Furthermore, at least twice a week you interpret the phrase 'balanced meal in the evenings' as meaning eight pints of bitter and a Kentucky Fried Horse.

In the same vein, you won't regularly restrict your baby's sleep in the evenings. If he drops off at any time the last thing you are going to do is wake the little bleeder up. Neither will you keep the baby to a regular routine of play time, bath time, blah-blah-blah. You know life doesn't work like that. If you are at a barbecue having a good time, you aren't going to rush home for your baby's bedtime. Even if you do, when you get home the hot water isn't on for a bath, you're too tired to consider any play and the baby has dropped off in the car anyhow. So you just try and slip him into the cot dirty nappy and all. Strict plans are useless. You won't keep to them.

The second reason that there is no 'Or your money back!' guarantee on this advice is . . . it won't work. Not much anyway. Some babies won't sleep much at night whatever you do. And that's the long and the short of it.

Actually, there is one thing you can do that will definitely work. But you won't do it, so I'm not going to tell you.

Nope.

Sorry.

Not telling.

Well, if you insist, I'll tell you in the next chapter. Even then you won't do it.

10

First Year:
You're a Baby Bore

Cocktail Chat

You didn't mention sex at all in the last chapter. Not once. You hoped this was appreciated. You thought it right that there was at least one sex-free chapter.

At every previous stage of the pregnancy the question has come up. Shortly after conception: sex okay at this point? Six months pregnant: sex still okay? You realised it sounded like you only had one interest. Not whether your partner was feeling well or the baby was developing correctly but whether any of this nonsense was going to interfere with your regular oats. (Your particular oats are the microwavable type – zero preparation time, two minutes on full power and you're done.)

Not so. Not you. There's no truth in the rumour that when you spoke to a midwife deep into the second stage of labour you said, 'My wife is ready for her epidural now and I wondered if we've just got time to slip in a quick bunk up.' Not even you were that obsessed.

But now it's been three months since you had carnal relations. That's twelve weeks, eighty-four nights or several boxes of Kleenex. The situation is becoming absurd. Your partner doesn't bother speaking the words 'not tonight, darling', she holds up a sign on a stick, which is useful because the perspex partition she's installed down the middle of the bed means you wouldn't be able to hear her anyhow.

What's going wrong? Well, if she had a very difficult delivery her vagina may still be quite sore. Also breast feeding can reduce a woman's libido and make it harder to achieve orgasm. (While solely breast feeding they probably won't start ovulating. It's a natural, though unreliable, form of contraception.) Add all this to the fact that she is physically very tired and you have a cocktail of negativity towards love-making. Not so much: 'Slow Comfortable Screw Against the Wall' as a 'Double Shot Of Brandy and a Lonely Hand Shandy'.

Joking aside, for some couples an extended sex-free period can develop into a serious annoyance. Tensions can rise and with them the problem gets worse.

Solutions include:

- Talking about the problem. Not only do you get to air your grievances and find out how she's feeling, you get to talk dirty.

- Try not to feel that your manhood is being threatened by not having sex. It's not personal. She didn't mind Mr Miniature with his tiny bowler hat beforehand and she doesn't mind him now.

- Believe her when she says her libido is reduced by breast feeding. It really is. Probably. At least, that's what they all say.

- Remember, she'll come around eventually. Eventually being the operative word. After six months it's perfectly acceptable to suggest it's about time you started thinking about a little brother or sister for your baby. Although one might consider this as putting out the fire with petrol.

- Try negotiating. If she says, 'Not tonight,' you say, 'How about one night next week, then?' If she says, 'I'm still too sore,' you say, 'There's more than one way to skin a cat and, since we're on the subject, there's a couple of cat-skinning manoeuvres I've always fancied giving a go. Miaow!'

- Try lubrication. While breast feeding, her juices may not flow so easily. This suggestion may not be easy to broach. A tub of lard on the pillow usually gets the message across without embarrassment.

- Have a drink to get you both in the mood. Beer goggles work equally as well on women as they do on men.

Mothering Sundae

One of the things couples do is look after each other. We all have the need both to mother and be mothered. Before a baby was on the scene your partner satisfied this need by mothering you. She would make you some nice little snack to eat, buy you a gift of socks or underpants, drag the duvet to the sofa for you when you are manfully trying to cope with your hangover and simultaneously trying to keep up with a full programme of events on *Grandstand.*

Equally your partner might scold you as a mother would: chide you for your farting, belching, swearing, laziness, leaving your dirty football kit in the hall, drinking, smoking, referring to her dad as an old toss-pot, snoring, dandruff scratching, leering, saying her mum has a fatter neck than Free Willy, making rude gestures out the car window, saying, 'Crikey Moses, you don't get many of those to the kilo,' whenever a large-chested woman walked by, not lifting the toilet seat, not putting the toilet seat back down, not replacing the toilet roll when it runs out, tearing pages out of her *Marie Claire* when there's no toilet roll, toe picking, teeth picking, ear picking, nose picking, bum picking, scrotum scratching and . . . and that's not the half of it.

On your side of the bargain you sated your mothering instincts by caring for her, buying her little extras, making sure she only had the best, doing her paperwork, cleaning her when she was dirty, keeping her well maintained, including tyre pressures, oil levels and keeping washer/wiper fluids topped up. Come to think of it, the time and money you spent on that car was another thing your partner complained about.

But it didn't stop you. You needed something to spoil. Even since your lovely baby was born you've kept on spoiling that vehicle. Loyalty means something to you.

Since this birth, however, your partner does not seem to have quite the same time to look after you. Or perhaps the truth is she doesn't have the same desire to look after you. Maybe . . . you don't want to over dramatise . . . but maybe, she now thinks of you with such contempt she is planning to have you killed.

Not only does she fail to spoil you so much, she can't even muster the energy to tell you off as much. It's true, at the time you complained bitterly about her constant complaining, but you sort of liked it. Now you could leave a sackful of sweaty jock-straps on the bread board and she won't mention it. You feel like begging, 'Please tell me off. I really need to be reprimanded for my boorish behaviour. Unless you nag me, how do I know you still love me? Without disapproval, I cease to exist.'

It comes down to this. You used to be the baby in this family and now a younger sibling has stolen your thunder. You became accustomed to being the centre of attention. Unchallenged, your antics guaranteed you top of the bill but now there is a new kid in town. He's cuter than you, he's more determined than you and, worst of all, he really is a baby. You might have done a pretty good cheeky-chappie Bruce Willis of a baby, but this newcomer is the Robert DeNiro of babyish behaviour. He owns the role. You, Bruce, better try auditioning for cheeky-chappie father roles or get used to all your performances going straight to video.

On the positive side, children eventually grow up and stop wanting to behave like infants. Smile sweetly at the child and bide your time. One day you can make a comeback.

Baby Development

Between three and six months old your baby has begun to fit into your lifestyle. A routine has developed of feeding, sleeping, bathing and changing. Your baby may still not sleep too great, but you've got used to a life dragging around in your dressing gown. Lowering your sights has meant that making it out to the corner shop for some wet wipes feels like genuine achievement, a cause for celebration almost. Funny how that shop always leaves your breath smelling faintly of alcohol when you come back.

Physically your baby will make rapid if unspectacular progress in this period. Whereas picking up a newborn is akin to holding upright an empty hot water bottle, by now it's like picking up a full hot water bottle, very full, so pumped up nothing moves at all. Arms and legs go straight out and refuse to bend. You become convinced that your baby could stand up he is so stiff. Unfortunately, he has the balancing capabilities of, say, a British Olympic gymnast.

Development progression runs as follows:

- one month – baby can hold head up a bit

- two months – can lift head slightly when lying down

- three months – can lift shoulders

- four months – can sit up if held steady

- five months – can push up on his arms

116

- six months – can sit without support but is likely to roll over
- nine months – can sit up and begin to crawl

The gradual process of automotive self-support is pretty similar to the progression you use when the alarm goes off on Monday mornings for work: head up, yawn, shoulders up, stretch the arms, big yawn, etc. etc. until you finally roll back over and think sod it, you'll tell the boss your car broke down on the A1.

Job Share

It's all very well sharing childcare with your partner but, ridiculously, society expects you to go to work as well. You spend half the night pacing around with the wakeful baby and your evenings trying to give your partner a break.

You stagger into the office most days like a punch-drunk moron. It must be affecting your performance. You hardly get any work done at all. Then again, you hardly ever did. But that was due to hard-earned indolence. Completing a few useful tasks in an eight-hour stretch took quite some effort. In those days you knew your obsessive skiving meant you suffered far more stress than even the company's top go-getters. Okay, those guys spent more time actually in the office but the time you spent doing sweet f.a. dragged so much that in purely human terms you were time-poorer. You knew, more than anyone, how painful clock-watching was. Resting on your laurels is far more strenuous than busting a gut, but, true to yourself, you stuck to the task.

Your current poor showing is entirely different. You really couldn't get much done even if you wanted to. (You still don't.) You are far too wasted and distracted to put corporate business first.

But try telling them that. They still ask you to work late three or four nights a week. Most weekends they intimate that everybody else is coming in on Saturday morning to help get that order finished ahead of schedule. Of course, it's not mandatory, comes the softener. The tacit threat remains, silent as a dog's whistle.

The boss has begun using phrases like, 'We cut you a lot of slack while your wife was pregnant but now it's time to get back to killing the opposition.' Or, 'We knew after the baby was born you needed a few days off but now you're a family man it's time to make your bid for promotion.'

Your 'bid for promotion' seems to mean doing whatever they say, whenever they say, for as long as they say and all to the neglect of your family. Your motto as family provider should be, according to them, 'Gotta work' as in, 'Sorry, darling, I know you're not feeling well and the baby is coughing, screaming, and covered in wet crap but I gotta go to work . . . Would you like another shot of vodka in your tea this morning?'

Maybe, in certain circumstances, if your baby has a life-threatening illness for instance, you can fight your corner. But try bursting into the MD's office and saying you can't get that urgent contract finished tonight because your little boy won't go to sleep unless you lie beside him on the bed and squeak the theme tune to *Pingu*. He will probably ask you to squeak the phrase, 'Can I have my P45 now, please?'

The government has introduced statutory entitlement to unpaid leave. Which is all very well but when the culture is 'going home is for wimps', who's going to take up their entitlement?

Maybe you will. Maybe as a new parent you are going to risk getting frozen out at work just when you need the job most. Looking on the bright side, maybe this work-crazy culture will change to accommodate fathers. When your boss had kids they thought a woman's place was in the home and their place was in the office. More importantly many of their wives thought so too. If a husband didn't come home on a Friday after midnight, completely kael-eyed, with a woman of loose morals on either arm, he was sent straight back to the pit to get some proper work done.

Back then, people had jobs for life. Now the working are expected to have jobs instead of lives . . .

You know all this because you were told it by your activist mate, Tom. Tom's recently turned twenty-nine and is halfway through a fifteen-year university course. He's planning to spend his late thirties alternating between the dole and trekking through India on the back of a yak. You suspect he's missing the point. Most jobs, once you get them sorted, can involve less effort than signing on for benefits. Also you are under the impression UB40 holders can struggle to secure a company car. He would probably be hard pushed to run a company yak.

Your action plan involves nodding agreeably to everything they say while thinking nasty swear words; finishing this damn contract to a standard that's borderline actionable; and saying you can't work tomorrow because you are a Jewish Quaker and every Saturday you have to go to the local mosque to flagellate yourself with a rasher of bacon.

118

Status Low

Bear in mind that work commitment whingeing won't cut much ice at home. Your partner is likely envious that you get to leave the house at all. Unless or until she goes back to work she might be feeling some loss of status as a housewife. She will certainly resent some loss of freedom being tied to a baby all day.

Of course some women take to motherhood like a duck to orange sauce. Bringing up baby makes them happy. They want nothing else. Apart from caring for you, possibly. Nothing can go wrong in this world. Not even that council application you've made to change the borough's name from Ilford to *Step*ford.

Baby Bore

Everything you've ever owned has eventually lost its sheen. Even that pet snake you had when you were twelve shed its novelty value quicker than its skin. Snake slithers, snake swims, snake reappears when mum's on the toilet. Yeah, so what? Even slipping the snake in your brother's baguette only got a laugh the first few times.

With a new baby, it's different. Once all the features have been explored and exhausted, it acquires a new set. The developments are constantly updating themselves as the weeks and months (and years) go on.

The fascination of watching your baby grow inch by inch and develop increment by increment is what the pleasure of parenting is all about. You will want to share this amazing development with the whole world and discuss it at length. This is natural. But don't be surprised if not everyone goes gaga over your baby's every goo-goo.

If you catch your friends stifling a yawn every time you relate the latest baby anecdote, take caution: you have turned into a baby bore. It's fine to be a baby bore in the right company, but only in the right company. For instance:

1 Your partner. She is the best person to share each moment with. The baby is hers too and she will never tire of talking about him.

2 Either set of grandparents. Finally you have a solution to all those awkward silences. Obviously you try to arrange to be out when your in-laws come around. At worst, you make sure you are never alone with them. But there is always that awkward five minutes while your partner goes to put the kettle on.

3 Any other new parents. Like the nice folk you met at the ante-natal classes. Shame you told your partner privately you thought they were all boring gits. Shame you made that pronouncement public via a postcard to them after the baby was born. 'Dear ante-natal class, Thanks for the flowers. Thank God we don't have to turn up again, ha-ha.'

People you should not 'baby bore' in front of include:
1 Single people. For them, babies hold no interest. You might as well be talking about your favourite side of the bed, or who gets up first to make the tea in the mornings, or what it's like to have someone else touch your genitals.
2 Couples without children. You know the scenario. In the past Keith and Jenny came around on a Sunday. You didn't bother to cook, but got a pub lunch, including several rounds of drinks. Then you all went back to your place, uncorked a couple of bot-tles of wine and looked at your skiing holiday pictures. At open-ing time you went back to the pub, had a few more drinks and began heavy drunken flirting with each other's spouses. 'I've always fawt you were a luvly girl, Jen. That bastard Keith treats you like a dusty dried-up bit of crusty old dog turd . . . He's always chatting up other birds, you know.'

Since you've had a baby, all this has changed. Keith and Jenny now come for 'high tea' at four o'clock. There's scones and tri-angle sandwiches and lashings of Lapsang Souchong. Pride of place in his brand new high chair is your new baby. You've altru-istically placed him right between Keith and Jenny so they can really get a good look at him sloshing his bottle of milk about (including spraying Keith's new Tommy Hilfiger T-shirt). When the baby regurgitates a couple of gallons of vomit down his bibby you cheerfully chuck Jenny the kitchen roll so she can have the honour of clearing it up.

Obviously there's no proper conversation at all. You are all too sober. Also you are much too interested in what sublime baby will do next. Any comments are solely in reference to the minu-tiae of baby's sleeping patterns, feeding patterns and poohing patterns. 'I must tell you, Keith, the contents of his nappy last week were amazing. The pooh was a greeny, whitey, yellow with rectangular lumps and a sort of coddled texture. Just like Chicken Korma. I've kept one of the nappies if you want to have a look. According to the books, it means he'll be an expert at maths.'

After the washing up is finished you suggest you all take a walk

up to the duck pond to throw some bread, but for some unfath-
omable reason Keith and Jenny decline. In fact, they already have
their coats on and say they must go home to get ready to go out
tonight. The rest of the skiing crowd are meeting down at a
trendy bar in the West End. Why not come along, if, heh-heh, you
can get a babysitter.

3 *Long-time parents.* This is where you get your own back on
Keith and Jenny. When, in a few years time, they finally get
around to having kids themselves, you will have a couple of
strapping toddlers. You've seen all these stages several times
before. As they launch into a Crouch End candle shop's worth of
wax-lyrical about their precious newborn, you can jokingly
demand that Keith should 'wake you up when he's finished with
a nice cup of tea'.

'I suppose you've been through all this,' Keith will say sheep-
ishly.

'Sorry Keith, no offence in your own house and everything,
but I have to inform you your baby is less endearing than the
Elephant Man and about as intelligent as broken house brick. My
kids were more advanced while still resident in my scrotum. The
decor was better too.'

Back Chat

You've heard about people talking to things that can't talk back:
coma victims, pets, plants, Gazza. (No offence, Paul. They just
happened to come out in that order.) You wondered how they
did it without feeling stupid. They did feel stupid at first, then
they got used to it.

You'll feel a bit silly talking to your baby at the beginning
but after a while it seems quite natural not to be answered
back (some would say quite a relief). A lot of people develop
'pet phrases' for babies. They can use these pet phrases in any
situation and on any baby. The trick is plenty of inane
repetition.

For example: 'Who's a pretty little sausage, then? Who's my
little sausage? Who's my itty-bitty sausage?' Alternatively: 'You're
saucy. Yes you are, you're saucy. Don't look at me like that, you
saucy little beggar.'

Try making up a few originals of your own. But if you're strug-
gling, here's a couple of ideas. 'Please make my shares go up.
Please make my shares go up. Please make my shares go up, 'cos
I want a Porsche.'

Or – 'You look like Boutrous Boutrous Ghali, you do. But nothing like Benjamin Netanyahoo.'

All this is very educational. Your baby will appreciate your attempts to communicate and return the effort. The development of speech goes roughly as follows:

Newborn baby – Neanderthal noises from the back of the throat – e.g. 'uuu' and sometimes 'aaah' and very occasionally 'Caaanton-naaah'.

Three months old – babbling noises – nothing specific but you can have a conversation of sorts with them. If you make a noise, they will return it. Even deaf babies babble.

Four months old – they begin to imitate sounds they hear you make from copying your mouth movements e.g. 'mmm-mmm' 'du du du'. In this period they also make strange clicking noises and other unusual sounds, noises that are used in other tongues. This explains the phenomenon of foreign babies being able to learn totally incomprehensible languages such as Swahili or Vietnamese. The Geordie accent remains a scientific mystery.

Six months old – proper words are still indistinguishable, but sounds are more like proper speech from your native country.

Ten to twelve months old – first words, e.g. Mama, Dada. Can also shake their heads to say 'no'. Saying 'yes' and nodding come along a lot later.

Beam Me Up Scotties

As I said there is one way to get your baby to go to sleep. Try this only with older babies, say nine months plus, who have a seriously non-sleeping problem. It's not my idea, but Dr Benjamin Spock's, the baby-rearing guru (the *Star Trek* bloke was *Mr* Spock). I mention this not because I want to share any credit but because you need to be reassured there is some scientific basis for the idea. He first published his *Baby and Childcare* book in 1946 and since then it has sold 50 million copies. (I'll be lucky if this sells half that.)

The theory behind the system is your baby cries in the night because it wants attention rather than anything else. Rather than pandering to that need in a namby-pamby new millennium way, you give it the cold-hearted 1946 treatment, i.e. ignore it and let it cry.

The details go like this:

First night – your baby will cry for thirty to forty minutes before eventually going back to sleep. This will seem like the longest half hour of your life and you'll almost certainly crack. But if you do, the game is up.

Second night – your baby will cry famously for about fifteen minutes before going back to sleep. This will seem like the longest fifteen minutes of your life. But if you didn't crack last night, you can probably cope.

Third night – baby cries for less than five minutes. This five minutes seems quite short. You are getting hard-hearted now. Huh! Five minutes! Is that all he can manage?

Fourth night – everyone, including the baby, has had enough of all this nonsense and he just goes back to sleep after a couple of minutes.

Fifth night – there is no fifth night because everyone's asleep.

No doubt during the leave-to-cry periods you will become convinced the baby is in some dire danger, head stuck between the bars of the cot, the string from the mobile tangled around his testicles. Dr Spock suggests, quite logically, captain, that this is unlikely. But if you are worried he advises you to find a way to peek into the nursery without the baby knowing. Not easy in the

1960s, but the modern world has provided us with video cameras (borrow one for three nights). It's simple to rig it up to view the cot and you can monitor it via a TV screen outside the room.

From personal experience, with a terrible crying baby for eighteen months, this worked in three nights. There were relapses, but the system did break the cycle of sleepless nights.

See, I told you you wouldn't do it. It seems cruel. It is in a way, but a physically exhausted parent is likely to be more cruel.

Crawling

At about six months your baby can get into a crawling position, but will refuse to move. You get down on all fours beside him and attempt the role of instructor.

'Come along, now. Off we go. One leg, two leg. One arm, two arm.'

Your baby grins at you but refuses to move. He's like an obdurate mule. Hmm . . . You get a couple of sugar lumps from the kitchen and place them a yard in front of your baby's nose.

'Come along, nice sugar lumps, lovely sugar lumps. One leg, two leg . . .'

The baby still refuses to move, so you crawl over yourself and sniff the sugar lumps, saying 'ooh lovely', until the dust from the carpet starts to make you gag. Nothing.

You move the lumps closer.

'Come along now, nice sugar . . . Come along, now . . . Mush! Mush!'

You move the lumps just a few inches from the baby's hand.

'All right, that's my last offer. If you can't even crawl that distance, the sugar is going back in the box.'

The baby tentatively reaches an arm out. Aah, you thought so. The right blend of carrot and stick was all that was needed. Maybe you do have management potential after all . . . Then, splat! Baby falls on his face. He starts screaming. Your partner runs in from the bedroom.

'He's all . . . right. He just er . . . rolled over.' This comes out rather mumbled as you're simultaneously trying to masticate two sugar lumps and a large tuft of Axminster.

The fact is babies will crawl when they are ready. For several weeks they consider their options but stay rooted in this all-fours position, possibly indulging in some gentle (though frustrating) rocking to and fro. Most babies should be crawling well by nine months.

11

Second Year, Second Child: Oh No, Not Another One

A Toddler's Gotta Do

Twelve months old is the beginning of the end of babyhood. Over the next year all membership credentials for babyhood – drinking milk, wearing nappies, crying and crawling – will lapse. Then it'll be time to clap a hand on your two-year-old's shoulder and say, 'You're a toddler now, son. It's time to turn into a foot-stamping, fist-beating, tantrum-screaming monster who shows us up in public places. It's a tough role that will test every ounce of your wilfulness. You probably know your mother and I will hate your guts for a whole year. But I think you're ready.'

But all that's to look forward to in the future. At a year, your baby will continue to keep the first three baby credentials for many months. Crawling, however, will soon cease, to be replaced by the upright biped motive system known as walking.

We take walking for granted. But a baby does not find it easy. From their perspective they've spent several months getting around perfectly happily on four 'legs'. It was a bit tough on the hands and knees but had the advantage of being extremely stable.

Suddenly he is expected to throw out the use of both front supports and simultaneously eschew using the solid round pads of the rear section so as to rise up to the bobbly rectangles at the end of their legs. These 'feet' seem altogether unsuitable for balancing. They are kind of flappy due to a hinge mechanism at the ankle. They are also miles away from the head, that weighty precarious boulder which is now terrifyingly far above the ground. It must be akin to an adult trying to run for a bus in a diver's helmet and twelve-foot stilts. Little wonder they wobble and crash down occasionally.

Somehow they manage, but in a few years will have given up this tiring business in favour of bicycles, skates and motorbikes before, at the age of maturity, returning to the quadramotive security of the motorcar. Home sweet home.

Curb Drill

With walking comes greatly increased freedom and, with that, new dangers. For example, once you let him walk down the pavement there's a chance he will run in the road. A very good chance. He does not understand that the clear, wide, tarmac area is reserved for cars while pedestrians have to make do with a donkey trail of uneven slabs that is variously obstacled with trees, wheelie bins, regular mounds of dog pooh and, of course, parked cars.

Several years ago there was a story of an infant child on a trip to the zoo. As his parents were distracted, the child ducked under a security rail and attempted to stroke a gorilla through the bars of his cage. The gorilla, after short reflection, responded by yanking the kid's arm off. The parents wanted to sue the zoo. At the time, before I had kids, I thought this was outrageous. It was clearly their own fault for not looking after their child properly. Now I know that a toddler can sprint away in seconds to become lost in a department store, run in the road, or sweep clean a sideboard of expensive ornaments in the home of a (former) close friend. I never found out if the parents won, but I do know Cherie Blair wants to represent the gorilla who is claiming both mental trauma and stomach upset from undercooked food.

One way to protect your child from the dangers of the road is to fit a set of reins, leather straps that fit around the waist. They are now considered slightly archaic but are still used widely in the rural communities where they harness several offspring to pull a trolley full of shopping, a plough, or to collect dad from the pub.

Bonnie Baby

Sitting on a park bench one day with your growing infant in the buggy, the woman next to you remarks what a 'bonnie baby' you have. Spare me the niceties, you think. If you're trying to say he looks plump just come out with it.

Later that day an old bloke in the butcher's shop begins making faces at your son and saying, 'Who's got chubby cheeks, then? You're going to grow up big and strong like your dad, aren't you.' You smile, but the 'chubby cheeks' euphemism does not go unnoticed.

That evening your mate, Alan, drops in for a drink. 'Don't take that kid to the seaside, he might get harpooned. What do you feed him on, live sheep?'

You realise you've just been spared the euphemisms. You should be grateful. Instead, you get defensive.

'No, we take a lot of care with his diet. He gets lean meat, salad, vegetables . . .'

'Yeah, all served in a sesame bap with large fries and a bucket of Coke. You do know you need planning permission for one that size. He needs to go on a diet.'

'Come off it, at that age their bodies are self-regulating.'

'Self-basting more like.'

'Leave it out, Alan, he's just bonnie.'

Obesity in children is becoming a problem worldwide. It is estimated that in the UK up to 22 per cent of children are overweight. In the US, the figure is even higher and the overweights tend to be much larger. So maybe if you emigrate there your child would be considered a lithesome waif.

If your child is obese (i.e. more than 20 per cent above normal weight for height charts) there are three main factors at work:

Heredity: fat parents often end up with fat kids. This may be due to unavoidable genetic factors, or because fat parents like to eat a lot and consequently regularly serve up gut-busting gastronomic blow-outs to their kids.

Diet: infants can be served too much fatty foods and/or sugary foods. A chocolate biscuit may be not be the healthiest solution to a crying baby. Mind you, it does tend to work and is a lot less effort than spending quality time with them after a hard day at the office.

Exercise: (that stuff they do on *Grandstand*.) Your infant has only just learned to walk so expecting him to do much sport is ridiculous. Anyhow, many tennis and golf clubs expect a certain standard of play before admitting members. On the positive side, any physical activity at all is useful in burning calories. I say all physical activity but you've learnt from bitter experience that certain pastimes carry hidden dangers: e.g. fridge-door opening, packet of biscuits unwrapping and even the rather strenuous ketchup-bottle shaking. (In the US, this 'Larder Triathlon' is seeking recognition as an Olympic sport.)

An example of a healthy daily diet for a toddler goes like this:

Breakfast: cereal with milk.
Lunch: small pieces of chicken or fish with potatoes and carrots. Fromage frais or yoghurt with fruit.
Tea: bread with cheese spread and slices of tomato.

You're thinking lunch sounds a bit of a handful. You could try rooting around the back of the cupboards for a jar of baby food. Life is a lot simpler when healthy diet merely involves rotating the colour-coded lids. A few baby jars in the diet can't do any harm. But they will need to be weaned off them before they take up full-time employment. A lunch pail made up entirely of mushy beans-and-chicken does not provide enough calories for the building site.

Fadding Time

Most infants do not suffer from obesity, but the fads and fancies of their eating habits do cause concern. You eat like so: sit down, cut and chew food in rotation, working steadily around the circumference of the plate until the last central morsel is eaten. Plate is clean. Job done. Five minutes have elapsed.

A child has its own method, normally requiring a minimum of an hour. Firstly, ignore food for at least fifteen minutes until completely cold. Then spend some time rearranging food around the plate, before widening the canvas to include the high chair, floor and large areas of the wall. Once this communist-style distribution is complete, they stand up in their high chairs to watch some TV. By the time *Telly Tubbies* is finished someone has usually reinstated their food as a single plateful, except now it is thoroughly mixed up and blended with a variety of household germs, cat fluff, etc.

Time to get down to the laborious task of eating. First mouthful enters the mouth, couple of chews, spit it out. Second mouthful, thirty or forty chews, then leave in the side of cheek. Remainder of food is utilised to devise interesting new game. Any words of encouragement from parent result in second mouthful being regurgitated sideways in direction of floor. Parent gives up and clears dinner away.

This method can continue seemingly for weeks without any evidence of food being consumed. It doesn't seem to bother them at all. Then one day a plate of food disappears within one minute flat. Eh? You can't believe they've eaten it all and begin hunting around for it, inside baby-gro, under high chair, down the back of the radiator. You try another plateful, and watch aghast as the baby actually begins to eat.

In other cases, appetite is restricted to a single food stuff, e.g. ham. The infant demands slice after slice of it with no let up. A family-sized bumper pack with forty per cent extra free is consumed within half a day. Fearing a diet of just ham is hardly balanced, you negotiate. If he will eat just one potato, he can have nine more slices of ham. The potato remains uneaten but the ham slips down a treat.

Rarely should these fads be a problem. Unless your child has become lethargic, it is getting all the energy and nutrition it needs. He has merely decided on the strange policy of eating only when hungry.

Upper Crust

You've listened to all the blowing and boasting until you were blue in the face. Every parent in the universe, without exception, has a baby that is both extremely advanced and genius-level bright. You've been informed how their little 'un was talking fluently at seven months or drawing with architectural lucidity at a year. You nod appreciatively, giving your best shot at pretending to be pleased for them, but frankly you couldn't be less bothered about all that competitive stuff.

Inside you are thinking: Oh my God, my kid's thick. Why me? Why did I have to be the one to end up with a baby who has a kilo of beef suet for brains? He'll be bullied at school, struggle to get a job and finish up on the scrap heap working at Spud-U-Like, or as a tyre fitter or, bloody hell, he could be one of those morons at the help desk at Homebase.

You come to this conclusion because all he can draw is scribbles, not even clever circular-form scribbles but a long wavy line that starts on the page but finishes halfway across the radiator, and the only thing he can say apart from 'mama' and 'dada' is the word 'pie'. That was because you once gave him some pieces of pork pie for lunch and he really, really liked it.

Everybody else has children who can say 'tractor' or 'fire engine'. One friend has trained his kid to respond 'Shakespeare' to any quote by him and 'Mozart' upon hearing any of the genius's music. What are you supposed to do in response, produce a piping hot Steak and Kidney from your pocket and demand: I bet you can't guess what this is, son?

You blame yourself. You were never that bright at school. You never revised for your exams. You have always avoided intellectual pursuits such as reading and painting, preferring to watch telly or if there's nothing on, go to the pub (come to think of it, in recent years you've begun going to the pub to watch telly).

Then it occurs to you. You are being a bit silly about the whole thing. Over-reacting, as usual. Blowing it all out of proportion. It's not your fault. It's nobody's fault.

Yes, it is. It's your partner's. She must have sullied your DNA with some dunce-capped genes of her own. All right, she has better exam results than you do, but that's only because she really worked hard for them. It's also true she does like reading and even paints once in a while. But it's easy if you're a woman. Women are allowed to do all that stuff without anyone thinking they are a bit of a wally.

You console yourself that in a few years your child will start school education. Then you can blame the teachers.

Keeping Up With the Studies

People exaggerate the accomplishments of their babies sometimes through rose-tinted false nostalgia and sometimes because they are horribly sad people who have taken to pathetically living their lives through their smarmy, know-it-all, hot-housed kids. Fortunately, you're not bitter.

The fact is children develop at different rates but mostly end up roughly the same.

IQ tests have been developed to measure this. The average IQ is 100 and 70 per cent of people fall within 15 points either side of this. Only 5 per cent fall more than 30 points either side (i.e. either above 130 or below 70).

The nature or nurture debate for intelligence is one psychologists have struggled to solve for decades. Genetics, or heredity, clearly plays some role. This has been proved by studies involving measuring the IQs of identical twins (who share exactly the same genetic blue-print) versus non-identical twins (who don't). The identical twins tended to have much more similar scores to each other than the non-identical twins. The conclusion drawn is: same genes, same IQ. So heredity appears to be a major factor.

But before you kick back and think, no point in bothering then, other studies have proved environment plays a large role. They took twenty pre-school kids from deprived families and gave them an 'enrichment programme' involving better nutrition, education and stimulation. Their IQs improved to over 100. A control group who were not given these advantages had an IQ that fell to an average of 65.

You wonder how it felt to be a parent in the control group. 'I'm proud to help with this scientific study by feeding my kid nothing but cardboard and letting him bunk off school. If we let his IQ rot down to single figures, we get a fifty quid bonus and a plastic carriage clock.'

IQ – DIY

You have begun devising a ten-point IQ test for babies. It's kind of clever, you feel, and you are confident it will be ready to unveil next time the Shakespeare-and-Mozart kid comes around with his dad.

Question One. What Greek letter is used to measure the area of a circle?

Question Two. What type of chart is regularly used in statistics?

Question Three. What was the Don Maclean song that began 'Bye-Bye, Miss American . . . ?'

Question Four. Let's see now . . . What Greek bloke had the surname Thagorus?

Question Five. Tum-te-tum . . . My favourite food is steak and kidney . . . ?

Question Six. Erm . . . Pork . . . ?

Question Seven. Erm . . . Erm . . . The opposite of 'hello' is 'good'? . . . Oh, forget it. He'll have to stay thick.

Development

Specialists divide child development into four areas: locomotive movement; hearing, understanding and speech; vision and fine movement; social behaviour and play.

The progression of skills varies enormously but all children acquire them in the same order, hence the phrase don't try to run before you can crawl. An approximate timetable is as follows:

131

One year old. Your child is crawling on hands and knees, walking around holding the furniture and starting to walk aided. Babies can grasp small objects and use both hands equally well, e.g. banging blocks together. They can respond when called by their names and can point to many household objects. They speak two or three words and like to play with adults familiar to them.

Eighteen months old. Your child will most likely walk well independently, including bending over to pick up objects. Babies walk upstairs but crawl down the stairs backwards. Dexterity-wise they can build towers of three blocks, turn the page of a book and scribble with a crayon. Preference to left of right handedness will begin to show. Vocabulary is still limited to about twenty words but they can understand most of what you say to them. Socially they are stubborn and cannot be reasoned with.

Two years old. Getting up and down the stairs on foot is now achievable. They can build a tower of six blocks and unscrew a lid. Their vocabulary has gone up to over fifty words and they can link two or more together in incomplete sentences. Socially they tend to be selfish about toys and prone to tantrums.

In other words your two-year-old is perfectly capable of

LOOK, I CAN'T TALK RIGHT NOW, BECAUSE, WELL.... I CAN'T ACTUALLY TALK YET !..

running up the stairs, grabbing a Tinky Winky out of your hand, and telling you 'Daddy, stupid bum' before throwing a wobbler. Beware, the language could be far stronger unless you are careful with your own.

Second Pregnancy

Along with everyone else you will never forget the first 18 film you got in to see at the cinema. Nobody remembers their second 18 film (apart from you, because it was a double bill). Again, like everyone else you will always remember the first time you had sex. But not the second. (Not even you dare to claim that was a double bill.)

It's the same with pregnancy and childbirth the second time around. All very nice, even quite exciting towards the end, but in years to come you probably won't remember much about it. A shame to think such an important landmark can fade into obscurity merely because it is the second one. Did Jackie Kennedy/Onassis feel the same level of shock when her second husband died?

'So Aristotle is dead. I see. That's fairly, um . . . awful . . . ish. I mean he was only seventy, which is quite young, in a way. He died in his sleep, you say. Which is a horrible way to go, I gather . . . Blimey, I'm famished. Must be the shock.'

Your partner's second pregnancy can go one of two ways. Chances are everything will be easier, mostly because you know what to expect. Those little mole hills you turned into mountains last time will this time be restricted to mere foothills. Slight worries always remain with any pregnancy. Of course, some people breeze through their first pregnancy: no sickness, no weight gain, no tiredness, no labour pain. A second pregnancy gives all their friends a chance to hope they'll really get it in the neck this time . . . '*Now* do you see what I went through?'

Your role as supportive birth partner in the second pregnancy is directed more towards looking after the older child. Any ill-effects your partner feels will be exacerbated by having to care for a demanding toddler.

I double-checked with my wife that there were no ante-natal classes to attend with a second baby. I was wrong. There were. So, too, with any subsequent babies. Somehow I must have missed them. Not on purpose. I must have been busy. Perhaps I wasn't pregnant, too, the second time. Maybe men get pregnant only once. So you better enjoy it.

Second Birth

The second time you go with your partner to see your new baby come into the world may not be so momentous as you are already a father. However, it should be a more enjoyable experience. You will be less anxious and so more able to take in the experience.

If you didn't fancy cutting the cord last time, this time you're willing to bite through it. If you were stuck up the head end with the first birth, this time you're heading straight for the coal face, your miner's helmet switched to full power and ready to winch open a jack between her knees. If you were too timid to demand the right pain relief, this time you'll be more assertive. 'Good evening, Matron, a bottle of your finest Pethidine, please, and make it snappy.'

Once the baby is born you'll be surprised at how few visitors you get. Oh, sure, the close relatives will show up – don't they always? – but the extended family stay out of the picture. Which is a relief. But somehow disappointing. This time you could have handled them. Since you've become more of a family man you've even come to quite like some of them. A bit. But most of them don't come to visit. The attitude seems to be ,'Oh, she's dropped another one, has she? You won't leave that poor girl alone, will you?'

If only they knew.

Second Baby

As discussed, the second pregnancy was something your partner felt she could handle much more by herself. The second baby 'suffers' from the same phenomenon. Now an old hand, your wife may want to take the lion's share of baby duties. You are left to look after the older one, at least initially.

Perhaps because of this, you could find the second baby less instantly loveable. You (like me) may feel it would be strangely disloyal to your first child for you to start loving the second one as much straight away. One solution is to make him serve a six months probationary period, during which time he can be sacked without notice.

'I'm sorry, son, it's a case of last in, first out.'

Clearly sacking is a bit harsh. But there's nothing to stop you withholding certain privileges of long service. Unfortunately this is easier said than done. You can't really send a three-month-old baby out to get the bacon rolls, nor ask it to work Bank Holidays. But, by Jove, you've got it. You won't let him join the lottery syndicate: any winnings for the first half year will only be split three ways rather than four.

One reason for this adjustment period where you withhold total membership is the old chestnut about the older child getting jealous. In my experience this does not hold water. The older child is much more adept at retaining (and demanding) yours and everybody else's attention. It's likely the new baby will have to play understudy.

One old cliché that is true is eventually you love all your children equally. And one day the lot of them will despise you for your old-fart equanimity.

12

Medical Section:
Bumps, Boils and Rashes

Clinical Trial and Retribution

You see yourself as a broad-minded fellow. You don't believe any of the old wives' tales about masturbation sending you deaf or blind or slowing your reactions.

Just to be sure, though, you've checked. You've run full clinical trials lasting more than a decade. The population sample maybe have been small – just a single person, actually – but the tests could not have been more thorough, and, what's the phrase . . . exhausting. Blimey, at times you hardly move afterwards.

The results are now confirmed. Your eyesight is still perfect although in the final throes you have been known to squint. Your hearing is also quite acute, particularly if you are trying to slip in a quick hand shandy while listening out for your partner returning from the shops. And as for those reactions, you're like Ben Johnson out of the starting blocks. At the first chink of a key in the door you can shut the magazine, zip up, return the magazine to the hiding place behind the wardrobe, wash your hands and compose yourself on the sofa with an (upside down) copy of *Captain Corelli's Mandolin* before she's made it down the hall with the first bag of shopping. Rather like Ben Johnson, your bulging bloodshot eyes and shifty demeanour may raise some suspicion but fortunately no one is going to subject you to testing.

SFX: Doorbell.

'Hello, sir, we're from the SWJTU. That's the Sneaky Wrist-Job Testing Unit. We need you to supply a specimen of your underpants.'

Cut to: Twelve months later. A courtroom.

'May it please your honour, my client insists the underpants became contaminated en route to the testing centre in Brussels. Even the prosecution concedes that to provide these levels, my client would need to masturbate a ridiculous eighteen times a day. He also contends the evidence discovered behind the wardrobe was planted. That's right, the pornographic material written entirely in Braille. Exhibits one to five hundred and forty-seven.'

The point is, to get back on the beaten track, even though you are a broad-minded chap, the sight of your toddler exploring its genitals can be disturbing. But many do so right from a very early age.

If you catch your child rubbing away, looking red faced and panting, he is probably masturbating. There is no sexual connotation to it. They do it because it feels nice and soothes them when they feel tired. It is not harmful, but there's no doubt it can be embarrassing as very young children may do it quite openly.

'No, no, the car's running fine, that squeaking is just my little Johnny in his child-seat bringing himself to orgasm . . . Now where shall I drop you, Bishop?'

Unless the masturbation becomes compulsive the best course of action is to hope it goes away, or divert their attention to something else. Obviously you should not make a lot of fuss or punish them.

Some kids play with themselves a lot, some don't at all, but in my experience the novelty seems to wear off by the time they reach nursery-school age. (No doubt to return one day.)

Ointment in the Fly

The chances are, over the next few years you will spend quite a bit of time in hospital waiting rooms. Every child ends up with their fair share of illnesses, ailments, cuts, bumps and breakages.

Certain children and, despite the risk of stereotyping, it seems to be mostly boys, end up with what only Robert Maxwell would describe as a fair share. They get their heads stuck in railings, fall off ten-foot climbing frames, and will prankishly swallow anything from a piece of chalk to an entire set of snooker balls. The first thing you know about it is when you catch their best mate lining up a break-off shot from the tip of your son's tongue.

The all-time classic is obviously getting the todger caught in their zip, clearly a very painful accident (see page 142). Sometimes no accident is necessary. As a young boy I decided to play hangman with mine. I tied a noose around his little head and strung him up to the side of the bunk bed much to the amusement of my sisters. Unfortunately it began to swell up and I had to go to hospital to get the string undone. A recent film dramatised this miscarriage of justice with Telly Savalas in the lead role and the Two Fat Ladies as my testicles.

Only kids know why they do these daft things. They wear off with age. When was the last time you cried off work because you caught your head in railings or your willy in your zip?

'Hi, boss, I'm afraid I'll be in late today . . . No, I promise I haven't got a hangover . . . Well, you see, I saw these railings on the way to the tube station and I just wondered whether they were quite large enough to . . . How can I put it . . . ? You hear that crackling noise? That's the fireman's oxyacetylene torch.'

Code Red

Waiting rooms are long established as the world's most boring places. It's bad enough having to take yourself off to the doctors or hospital and every additional child you have ups the quota. Many hospitals make efforts to reduce the stress by giving babies and children a higher priority. Some provide separate waiting rooms that contains a box of broken old toys and several battered books. This helps a bit. But in the end taking your kids up the hospital is just part of what being a parent is all about. You give them your time and your patience and your love. Console yourself that once they are old enough they will comprehend all you've done for them and give thanks. Mind you, any appreciation will be delivered in code.

'Thanks for all you did for me as a kid,' may be translated into the teenager language of 'I never asked to be born.'

'I hate you, Dad, you fat old git' easily translates back to 'I really love you, Dad, you fat old git.'

'I going to buy a shotgun, blow you to pieces and then gladly go to prison for it' . . . actually means 'I'll shoot you dead and claim it was an accident and anyway no jury would convict after the way you've mistreated me, you drunken bum.'

Dr Mickey and Dr Donald

On a serious note, you will spend much time worrying about minor illnesses in your children. This worrying does decrease with experience and the number of children you have.

But how do you tell, particularly as a first-time parent, what is minor and what is not? Very difficult. You will clearly think better safe than sorry. A schlep up to the doctors' surgery, or casualty, or the awkward weekend call to the GP should never be avoided or put off.

The general danger signs of serious sickness are as follows:

- Child is unusually sleepy or listless
- Has breathing difficulties
- Feels very hot
- Becomes dehydrated – by persistent vomiting or diarrhoea or refusal to drink any fluids
- Looks very pale and has a cold sweat
- Cries with severe pain

Instinct, Basically

Parents know instinctively when something is seriously wrong. Trust your instincts. If you feel your child needs to go to hospital for tests, take him. Don't let some overworked or jaded GP put you off. Just as you did for your wife in childbirth, you need to stand up for your child.

Vaccinations

Taking a baby to the doctors for an injection is not much fun. Holding their leg still while a doctor or nurse sticks a huge great needle in them is distressing. You could steel yourself by thinking of all the times the screaming brat has kept you awake at night.

The current UK schedule for vaccinations is as follows:

Approximately 8 weeks old – Tetanus, Whooping Cough, Hib, Diphtheria, Polio.

Approximately 12 weeks old – Second course of Tetanus, Whooping Cough, Hib, Diphtheria, Polio.

Approximately 16 weeks old – Third course of Tetanus, Whooping Cough, Hib, Diphtheria, Polio.

After the three sets of injections, babies will invariably become slightly feverish in reaction to the immunisation. The doctor will probably advise you to give the baby infant Calpol.

In the second year your toddler will be immunised for Measles, Mumps and Rubella (MMR).

What Is All This Stuff?

The names of most of these immunisations will be familiar to you. What the diseases are and why they are so dangerous may not.

Diphtheria – a serious throat infection that can fatally obstruct breathing.

Polio – a virus that can cause paralysis.

Tetanus – an infection from dirt in cuts. Can lead to breathing failure.

Whooping Cough – spasmodic coughing, can't catch breath.

Measles – rash, fever, vomiting, cough – can cause pneumonia and encephalitis (brain inflammation).

Mumps – swollen glands in lower jaw. Generally this is not too serious for a child but if caught by men in adulthood can affect the testicles and cause sterility.

Rubella – a virus commonly known as German Measles. Again not too bad for a child but is very dangerous if caught by pregnant women – i.e. possible birth defects.

Hib – stands for Haemophilus Influenza type B – a virus that can cause meningitis.

General Medical Advice

All the usual dull warnings apply about not relying on this advice, but checking with a doctor to be sure. For some reason the publishers' lawyers didn't think my CSE grade 7 in Biology entitled me to give unswerving medical diagnoses. Not even my certificate for swimming 10 metres in my pyjamas could sway them.

Asthma – allergic condition caused by dust mites, pollen, pets, certain foods etc. etc.

Symptoms: wheezing, coughing, breathing problems, particularly at night.

Treatment: medication either by syrup or inhaler. No cure but most kids grow out of it.

Chest infection – inflammation of lungs caused by a virus.
Symptoms: fever, coughing (sometimes with phlegm), breathing problems, vomiting phlegm.
Treatment: keep warm; plenty of fluids; for bad coughs see a doctor, encourage productive coughing, antibiotics may be prescribed.

Chicken pox – highly infectious virus, can be dangerous for very young babies.
Symptoms: high temperature; small red blisters/spots starting on the torso then spreading to the rest of the body.
Treatment: calamine lotion for spots; try to stop the child scratching them (a lot easier said than done) as they may scar, although any scars will fade quite a lot; see a doctor if scabs become infected or fever starts.

Choking – body's attempt to clear something stuck in the airway.
Symptoms: coughing, spluttering, going blue, losing consciousness.
Treatment: children do this a lot, and normally they can clear the object themselves. Unless child goes blue, he is getting oxygen which is the main worry. Slap child on the back several times to dislodge the object or hold him upside down. Call ambulance if child loses consciousness even for a short time.

Colic – stomach pain of uncertain origin but common in babies.
Symptoms: persistent crying, particularly after feeding, drawing up of knees, baby seems full of wind.
Treatment: very little; try gripe water; but mostly just do your best to comfort the child and cope with the crying.

Constipation – hard pooh getting stuck and refusing to shift.
Symptoms: empty nappy.
Treatment: plenty of fluids; don't worry too much as babies tend to be irregular; if there is bleeding call a doctor.

Cot Death (Also SIDS, or Sudden Infant Death Syndrome) – most likely between ages of two months and two years. Still largely unexplained but theories abound, most likely respiratory failure in response to some trigger.

Prevention measures (latest advice): put your baby to sleep on his back, make sure he does not get too hot (i.e. if you feel much too hot so do they); no pillows under one year, no smoking in the house, breast fed babies show less incidence of cot death.

Croup - inflammation of vocal chords.
Symptoms: barking cough; wheezing; breathing problems.
Treatment: keep air moist by boiling a kettle or sitting child in a steamy bath. Let child sleep in more upright position. See a doctor.

Eczema - allergic response similar to (and often hand in hand with) asthma.
Symptoms: dry, itchy rash on face, neck, hand and creases of the skin.
Treatment: medications range from creams, soaps and syrups. Other treatment include special diets and using cotton clothing. Many children grow out of it.

Fever - Rise above normal body temperature (98.6°F/37°C) resulting from virus or bacterial infection.
Symptoms: hot forehead; aching joints, loss of appetite, hot and cold spells.
Treatment: check with doctor, drink plenty of fluids, infant paracetamol (Calpol or other) to reduce temperature.

Glue ear - thick gluey fluid build-up in the middle ear.
Symptoms: earache, partial hearing loss.
Treatment: see a doctor. Antibiotics may be prescribed; some-times fluid is drained by tiny surgical incision in the ear drum; grommets are placed in the ear to stop fluid build-up.

Measles - highly contagious virus, with potential for complica-tions.
Symptoms: runny nose, dry cough, fever, tiny white spots on inside of cheeks, followed by dark red rash spreading from face to body, deliriousness.
Treatments: see a doctor, fluids, rest, lots of nursing, possibly antibiotics.

Meningitis - two types, viral and bacterial, the latter being the most dangerous. Inflammation of the lining of the brain.
Symptoms: initially similar to flu, hence the problems diagnosing

the illness, which if delayed may lead to death. Symptoms different to flu are: intolerance to bright light, fever with cold hands and feet, stiff neck, a rash which when pressed under glass does not disappear.
Treatment: call doctor urgently, or visit casualty immediately. Bacterial meningitis can be treated with antibiotics.

Nappy rash – skin inflammation due to contact with dirty or wet nappy.
Symptoms: red inflamed skin in nappy area.
Treatment: antiseptic nappy cream (e.g. Sudocream), leave nappy off to let air get to skin, change nappy frequently.

Penis Stuck in Zip – self explanatory.
Treatment: if actual penis is caught (rather than just skin) take child quickly to hospital, numbing pain with ice-bag. When only the skin is caught, try cutting out the zip and unpicking it from the bottom. If this fails take child to hospital.

Sticky Eye – inflammation of the eye common in most babies immediately after birth but for some remains for months afterwards.
Symptoms: yellow discharge around the eye.
Treatment: try cleaning around eyes with cotton wool for a few days, using separate ball for each eye. If this fails go to doctor for some drops.

Swallowing things – for objects see *Choking*; for medicines, alcohol, solvents or poisonous plants, see below.
Treatment: ring doctor or ambulance, do *not* attempt to induce vomiting by giving very salty water as this can be fatal to a young child; instead give milk to dilute the poison or try sticking a finger down their throat. Take the child to hospital with a sample of whatever swallowed. If the child is unconscious, attempt resuscitation making sure to avoid getting any poison in your own mouth.

Teething – takes place at intervals between five months and three years.
Symptoms: irritability, dribbling, red cheeks, swollen gums.
Treatment: gel for the gums (e.g. Bonjela), infant paracetamol for severe pain, stuff to chew on (e.g. teething rings, special hard teething biscuits, bits of apple).

13

Financial:
Baby Boom or Bust

The Sport of Money

Perusing the Sunday newspaper you accidentally flip over two pages past the racing results to the financial section. You glance at a couple of headlines: Russian and British Treasuries To Merge . . . yawn. . . . Entire European Gold Reserves Mislaid By Caretaker . . . yeah-yeah . . . Interest Rates To Quadruple In Six Months Says Gordon Brown . . . Who? Oh I remember, the bloke who did the *Krypton Factor*.

Do people actually find any of this stuff interesting? Why wade through all that when there's a 2,000-word interview with a Liverpool ball-boy on the previous page?

Then a large advertisement catches your eye.

Advertisement
FREE MONEY DIRECT!
We guarantee to transform your finances: *cut* your mortgage in half, *slash* life insurance by 60 per cent, *scythe* your tax bill down to the bare earth, *shave* household bills, *wash, trim, and blow dry* interest payments and erm . . . *nip a couple of inches* from your bank charges. All this in one simple two-minute phone call. Call Free Money Direct!

Free Money Direct, eh? . . . Nah, can't be bothered.

Even the phone call is free: dial 0800 then hit any key. It's that simple!

No thanks.

One more thing: there's no strings, no ties, no lock-in periods, no nothing and the first 60 callers win a tax-free lump sum bonus on retirement.

Look, pal, I don't care. It's my day off, okay.

When it comes to financial planning you must be the most apathetic bloke in the world. Meanwhile banks, building societies and insurance companies are getting very rich at your expense. Where do you think they get the money for the multi-million pound executive pay-offs? They rely on your apathy so they can rip you off. They get a golden handshake by giving you a golden shower.

Sorry, did you say something? I must have dropped off.

You are not alone. We all do it. Reasons for apathy run as follows:

- *Financial planning is too complicated.* Yes, it is. A lot of companies make it so on purpose to stop you changing from their expensive product to a cheaper one. They make you fill in forms, apply for documents, and have a whole array of technical small print that makes it hard for you to move.

- *Finance planning is too boring.* Not really. Saving and earning yourself money is brilliant. It's just the filling in of forms etc. that is tedious.

- *Financial planning is for the birds.* None of us can imagine being old, or ill, or dying. (This is true in your case; that diet of beer and fried food you live on is the secret of eternal youth.) But even if you do decide to plan ahead, those wily financial advisors like to nick a couple of years payments for their commission.

Duty Calls

Most men shoulder the responsibility for family financial decisions. That's why advertisers of big ticket products like cars and insurance policies generously support the most minor of TV sports. It's also why double-glazing salesman call around in the evenings.

'Excuse me, madam, is your husband in?'

'I'm sorry, he's at work.'

'That's a shame. I need to sell him a useless product that's so shoddily installed we end up in a five-year legal fight.'

'Oh right. Well, he should be back about six thirty.'

Yes, you are the one who has to take the flak for purchasing dodgy conservatories, second-hand cars and time shares. This is the role that gives you the status as 'head' of the family. Your partner may wear the trousers, but you have to make sure the pockets are empty.

Becoming a family man has provided a host of financial opportunities you can make a mess of. Your position has changed on tax, benefits, insurance and household costs.

Knowing what your position is on all these things can save you money, or at least protect you from losing more of it. Fifty per cent of the battle is bothering to do anything about finance. Another 50 per cent is knowing your rights. The last 50 per cent is making sure all the figures add up.

Being a dad doesn't mean you have to become horribly sensible all the time, not even some of the time. Once in a while will do. There are a several things you can do to improve your financial position and the security of your family. Some take almost no effort, some take a bit more effort and a few . . . no, forget those.

Below are some thumbnail sketches of things that might help. I wouldn't bother to read them if I were you.

Married and Unmarried Income Tax Allowance

If you are married you already receive the Married Man's allowance on top of your personal allowance. The value of this is arrived at by, surprise, surprise, a circuitous route but basically ends up at about £197 less tax per year. That's £16.50 a month. Not brilliant, but enough to cover your satellite subscription.

What some people don't know is you become entitled to this allowance even if you are *unmarried* – once you have a child. It's called the Additional Personal Allowance. You have to claim it, though, either through your tax return if you are self employed or by calling the Inland Revenue and asking for form 11-PA. You then merely sign a declaration to state when the child was born and your PAYE tax will be reduced. You have to do this yourself. Your employer can't make the declaration on your behalf.

Child Benefit

This is currently (1999) worth £14.40 per week for the first child and £9.60 for each subsequent child. You have to claim it though. If you forget, they will only backdate the claim for a maximum of three months.

To claim, call the Child Benefit Hotline on 0541 555 501 and ask for a claim form. Once received you will have to send the baby's original birth certificate (which they will return to you).

Any money is automatically paid to the mother unless she signs a declaration allowing it to be paid to you.

Inheritance Tax

If you die all your money and assets go to your wife with no tax to pay (and vice versa). But only if you are *legally married*. Otherwise the Inheritance Tax allowance (in 1999) is restricted to £223,000 worth of cash and assets. If you have, say, an insurance policy to pay off your mortgage, you might go over this figure. In this case, your common-law wife would pay 40 per cent in tax on the excess.

If both you and your partner die, the same Inheritance Tax allowance restriction applies when your estate goes to your children. However, you and your partner/wife each get an allowance (which may be a good reason for having a house in joint names).

Maternity Benefits

Your wife or partner is entitled to Statutory Maternity Benefit from her employer if she has worked for them for more than 26 weeks. The rate is (in 1999) 90 per cent of her salary for six weeks, then £57.70 a week for 12 weeks.

Unemployed or self-employed women are entitled to SMP at £51.70 per week for 11 weeks before birth and six weeks after. (Call 0181 258 8855 for details.)

Paternity Benefits

No such luck.

Wife's Personal Allowance

This is not transferable to you. Which doesn't seem fair to me, when you are supporting her while she gives up work to look after the kids. Why should double-income families get a tax advantage? The reason: nobody complains.

However if you are self-employed, there is nothing to stop you employing your wife (or partner) and using up her allowance of £4,335. This would save you nearly £1,000 in tax. Be certain the job would seem bona-fide in the eyes of the Inland Revenue. Giving her £80 a week just to post the odd letter might seem dubious, even if the post box is a 'good five-minute walk'.

She needs to be a book-keeper, or telephone receptionist. Better still make her your secretary, then begin a clandestine day-time affair with her, threatening to restrict her promotion prospects unless she performs certain 'extra-curricular' activities in the afternoons.

Children's Tax Allowance

Yes, even kids get a full personal allowance of £4,335. But will probably need to become baby models to earn it. (That's supposed to be a nightmare, by the way. Low pay, short career and every co-star a tantrum-meister.) You would have a hard job convincing the Revenue your six month old was Chairman of the Board.

Benefits

The rates of Job Seekers Allowance change all the time but are roughly £100 a week for a couple with a child.

Obviously you have to apply for these by means of filling out several forms and answering literally hundreds of questions. It's a real pain. But if you end up unemployed, do it immediately rather than put it off. They won't backdate any money on the grounds that you never got around to it.

Life Insurance

If you have a mortgage you will certainly already have some life insurance to pay it off. It may be part of your endowment policy. You might want to take out additional life insurance for you and/or your partner to support surviving dependants. Alternatively, you can insure your partner's life for the cost of child-care while you are at work.

Private Health Care Insurance

If you have a company scheme check if your wife/partner and children are covered under it.

Private Maternity Care

Run-of-the-mill pregnancy is not covered under insurance schemes like BUPA. If you want to go private, you have to pay for it. Each night in hospital can cost £300. The cost , in 1999, of having a baby at the trendy Portland Hospital like Posh, Scary, Fergie and the rest is approximately £7,000.

Medical insurance schemes do pay out if there are medical complications which need special procedures (e.g. a Caesarean). They won't pay out just because you are 'too posh to push'.

Childcare

The cost of childcare is not tax deductible. If your partner wants to return to work she must weigh up the fact that her net income must cover the gross income, including tax and National Insurance, of a nanny, childminder or nursery place.

However, childcare is tax free if provided free by an employer at the workplace. Not many companies currently provide this facility but a few do (e.g. one bank heavily subsidises the cost and this subsidy is tax free).

Costs Of Bringing Up Baby

Strange to think people are far more willing to plan for things that are very unlikely to happen than what probably will. The likelihood is that you won't die in a plane crash, or have your legs crushed under a bus but will live on day to day trying to support a family. Unless you are the type of weirdo who started saving for a baby years ago there's not much you can do. You cannot insure yourself for the cost of pregnancy.

You could put some money away for a rainy day, though, or school fees or for a second child. Each child is estimated to cost £100,000 in food and clothing. Private education would cost the same again on top. Faced with this, you might decide to keep the cash for new cars and flashy summer hols and put up with having a thick kid. No guilt required. You figure a happy, tanned, relaxed parent with a wicked motor is a good parent.

There are a million and one ISAs, endowments and saving schemes to help you to save. Stick a small amount away each month and forget about it. Check the charges and commissions levied before doing so.

If this sounds way too boring, try Premium Bonds. They pay

no interest but do give regular small winnings and could provide a million-pound jackpot.

More dubious investments include doing the lottery, gambling on horses, or starting your own wine cellar comprised entirely of rare sub three-quid-a-bottle Soaves.

By all accounts, the most efficient way of saving money is to pay off your mortgage quicker. Again, those friendly banks normally discourage you from doing this, because they are making money out of you. Consider a flexible mortgage. Then you could pay a bit more off now and a bit less when you have another kid.

Conclusion

So, you were pregnant too, mate. How did it feel? Do you view the world through the eyes of a changed man? Does quiche taste any better? Are you now Mr Empathy when it comes to your partner's feminine needs?

When she says: 'Not tonight, darling. I'm having my period.'

Do you reply: 'Apologies, dearest. How remiss of me not to keep track. Let me furnish you with a winged absorbent pad for your gusset, a hot water bottle for your stomach cramps and afterwards I shall retire to the back bedroom where I can relieve my own base needs in solo mode'?

Once a woman has been through pregnancy, labour and delivery she feels she has completed life's toughest triumvirate of physical experiences. In doing so, she has passed through to a higher level of womanhood. So women have pregnancy and men have to make do with drinking a yard of ale.

In birthing up a fully fledged baby your partner has traversed the full spectrum of her emotional resilience from incredibly brave to horribly scared. Few blokes can claim quite the same.

'Yes, pal, I felt a bit gippy when that dirty great liver-and-onions thingy popped out, but apart from that it was a breeze.'

But in truth this is macho posturing. During pregnancy and particularly birth the old emotional speedometer nudges the red at times for men too. We don't actually get to give birth (thank God), but were so closely involved as to make little difference. Our vicarious experience of pregnancy can be profound as long as we are paying attention.

Having passed from mere coupledom into the responsibilities

of family life there's no doubt we face many more sacrifices than we imagined. Probably a lot less sex for one thing. Certainly a lot quicker sex.

Husband: 'Oh Lord! You red hot sex bitch. I'm so hot for you.'

Wife: 'Hurry up and get finished before the kids come in.'

You have to start to watch your language too. Otherwise your children may assume that taxi drivers are not called taxi drivers but known as 'kin-wanker-cutmeups'.

Sex and swearing are two of life's major pleasures but you still have football, boozing and watching telly. Once they are a little older your kids will whole-heartedly share in your juvenile enjoyment of belching, farting and generally playing the goat.

Having children means the selfishness of youth too must be largely sacrificed. However I believe it's vital to retain some selfishness and live for ourselves too. Otherwise we rapidly descend into Saturday night sherry-sipping, Sunday morning car-washing drones. Then we are just a premature wrinkle away from deciding beige nylon slacks with a cream safari jacket are the height of fashion and Bournemouth is the new Ibiza.

To this youth-retaining end, a few years ago I decided I was for once going to forget about family prudence and treat myself to something special.

At the time I was working very hard and earning a decent amount of money. The monster of the family budget swallowed up most of it, but with careful planning (i.e. hire purchase) I could afford my personal treat, a brand new sports car.

A sports coupé to be precise, the sexy new shape Honda Prelude 2.2 VTEC. Its exterior curves oozed sexuality (mine no longer did. A stone-cold certain fact of parenting is you get fatter!). Inside, along with the ridiculously cheesy sub-Thunderbirds blue neon dashboard, the Prelude was a cramped four-seater. Still I worked out I could just about fit in my small children, allowing the car to be at least vaguely practical.

Being me, I procrastinated several weeks about lashing out such a large sum of money. In the meantime I visited or telephoned every Honda dealer in England for the best deal. Furthermore I checked every statistic and specification available about this car. I bought not just *What Car?* magazine, but *Which Car?*, *Why Car?*, *When Car* and *Bleeding Hell Get On With It Car*.

Finally, sick of my own pussy-footing, I strolled into my local dealer, barked a greeting at a greasy amphibian salesman and slapped my credit card on his smoked glass table.

'One Honda Prelude 2.2 VTEC in diamond black please.'

His lizard tongue protruded a moment before he swiped a £500 deposit on my card and handed me a sheaf of order papers. With that I drove home to break the news to my wife. Finally, I had held my nose and stumped up my cash.

'How big is this car?' she asked.

'Big enough. There's no proper leg room in the back but you could just about fit two small kids in it.'

'What about three small kids?'

'No chance, it's a two plus two. Oh, but you've got to see this amazing dashboard . . . Hang on, a minute. What do you mean, three small kids? Oh no, please, no.'

But oh yes. Six months later I was to become a father for the third time. There was to be no sexy sports coupé, no Thunderbirds dashboard and no special present all for me.

Instead, I had a healthy little daughter. Once I got over the shock and silly disappointment, I realised she was much more valuable and important and would bring me far more joy for a much longer period. I love her very much. In no way do I blame her for losing my treasured Prelude. She still bloody owes me that £500 deposit, though. Which means no pocket money until 2009. That's only fair, isn't it?

Instead of sports car swanking, I've had to make do with a few more years of life in a rusty beige Volvo and wearing sick-stained suits. Maybe that puke stripe across the shoulder will become trendy one day. I doubt it, though. Having children is anything but glamorous. It is the antitheses of such because glamour is about myth with surface glitter. Having children is about reality, pungent as Camembert, gritty as a whelk's swimming trunks.

Pregnancy must be the training for this return to reality. All a couple's white lace pretensions are shed. Now you know your partner bleeds and shits and pisses just like you do. You've been through a lot together. You've worn the T-shirt and rinsed out the knickers too.

If pregnancy was a game of football, it was an over-tense cup final. The game was a long one lasting nine months rather than ninety minutes, the overdue time lasted two weeks not half an hour, the resolution needed a long night of labour rather than ten kicks from twelve yards. There were no winners, no losers, no Germans or Argentineans, no Russian linesmen, and no Nobby Stiles, and the only Stuart Pearce-esque exclamation came during conception.

Pregnancy felt at times like a very long nil-nil draw but eventually a hugely satisfying one. You were playing away from home, pregnancy is still very much women's turf, but still managed to come away with a well-earned result. Well done, mate. Take a short break then start preparing for coming back to Wembley again next year. One baby often leads to another.